dish
entertains

trish magwood

dish
entertains

everyday simple
to special occasions

HarperCollins*Publishers*Ltd

Dish Entertains
© 2007 by Trish Magwood. All rights reserved.

Published by HarperCollins Publishers Ltd

First Paperback Edition

HarperCollins books may be purchased for educational, business, or sales promotional use through our Special Markets Department.

HarperCollins Publishers Ltd
2 Bloor Street East, 20th Floor
Toronto, Ontario, Canada
M4W 1A8

www.harpercollins.ca
www.dishcookingstudio.com

Library and Archives Canada Cataloguing in Publication

Magwood, Trish
dish entertains : everyday simple to special occasions / Trish Magwood.

ISBN: 978-1-55468-437-3

P+ 9 8 7 6 5 4 3 2 1

Photography: Brandon Barré
Additional photography: Erin Riley, pages 5, 11(middle, left and bottom, centre), 16, 25, 31, 33, 35, 39, 49, 78, 91, 100, 117, 147 (top), 161, 171, 187, 188, 217, 219, 229, and 234-235
Printed and bound in China

dish

for my family—

four generations of good cooks and happy eaters

acknowledgements

This book is dedicated to my family: my grandparents, with whom I shared count-less meals; my mom and dad, who still bring our growing family together for every possible occasion; Bryce, my patient supporter, sous-chef and party co-host, and his family; my brothers Tim, Jeff and Robbie and their spouses Nancy (Ryan, Sophie, Zac), Amy and Amanda, who collectively carry on the tradition of gathering around food (and lots of drink) for every milestone; and our children, Olivia and Findlay, whose favourite place is in the kitchen, where all the action happens.

  dish entertains is in part a reflection of all the dish chefs and our stories. They are a high-energy, vibrant and dynamic group of experts from whom I learn every day. To our chefs, Sacha, Elena, Charmaine, Andrea, Joshna, Brooke, Michelle, Lisa, Kris-ten, Gillian, Adell; to the party planners and client service pros, Pam and Alynn; and to the rest of the team: dish is a success because of your passion, spirit and shared vision. Mom, Nancy, Stewie, Amanda, Bay and Martha, my dedicated testers and sea-soned home cooks, I'm grateful for your invaluable input into every recipe. To Sacha, for the beautiful food styling and for undertaking this project with me. To Andrea, for sticking by me and Elena, for your loyalty and being the queen of the kitchen. To Brandon along with Cory for turning my creative vision into truly beautiful pictures that exceeded my expectations; Erin and Kitty for your contributions to the look of dish; Al and the *party dish* gang for helping to bring dish to life through *party dish*; and my old friends Tori, Foofie, Bay, Lisa, Kristi, Sarah, Lynn, Becky, Dayna and Rahat.

  The true experts are our suppliers: Stanley at Whitehouse Meats; Danny at Harvest Wagon; the boys at Alex Farms; Afram at The Cheese Boutique; Mark at St. James Steak & Chops; my dad, a budding farmer; and Charles Baker (Stratus Wines). All the supportive restaurant chefs who have taught at dish: Greg Couillard, Massimo Capra (Mistura), Jamie Kennedy (JK Wine Bar), Matt Sutherland (Fat Cat), Rod Bowers (Rosebud), Lynn Crawford (Four Seasons), David Lee (Splendido) and Claudio Aprile (Colborne Lane).

  So many people have helped me along the way: Michael de Pencier, Peter Oliver, George Butterfield, Mary Risley, Jack Creed, Al Magee, Karen Gelbart, Tanya Linton, Linda Haynes, Mary Crothers, Allison Fryer, Kirsten Hanson, Alan Jones and the team at Harper Collins and my brilliant and unflappable business advisor Paula Jubinville. Why is it that the busiest people are always the ones who make the time to help? It's true the sum is greater than its parts.

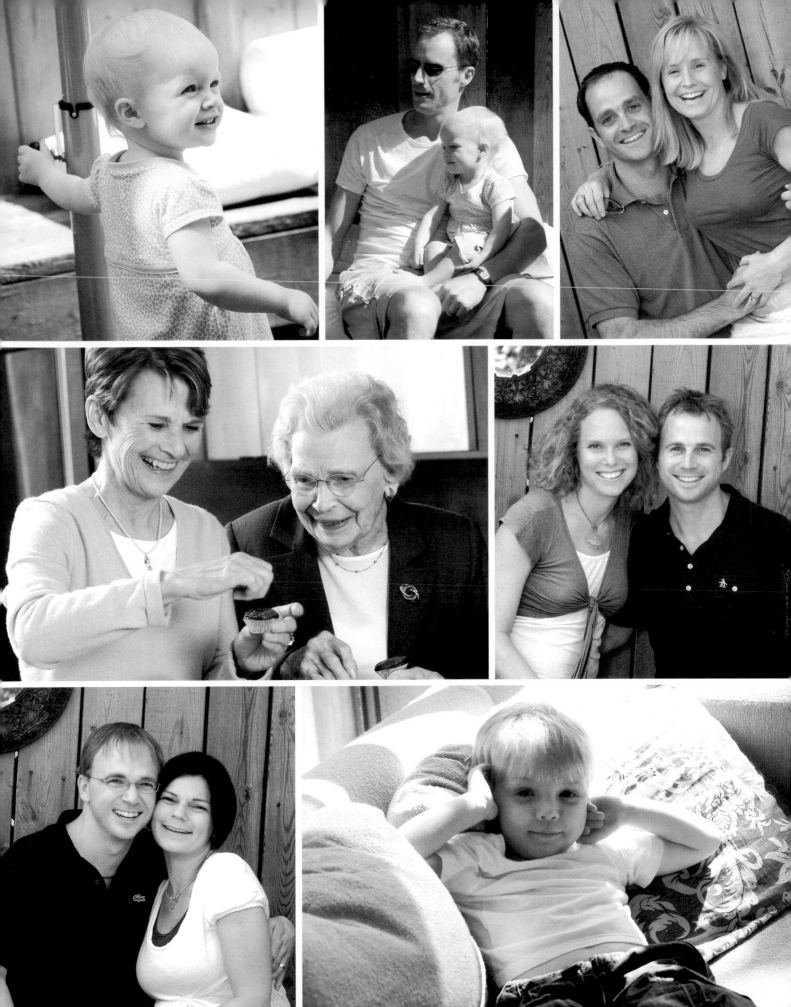

table of contents

the dish story

In my home, food has always been shared around the family table. Food is the medium through which family and friends connect and come together. My mom and grandmother instilled in me the importance of time spent cooking. For them, as for me, cooking is the best way to express appreciation and love. This book represents that same passionate tradition of food and togetherness, only within the time-squeezed reality of contemporary life.

I suppose I have always tried to connect with people through cooking. As a young cook for fifty hungry tree-planters in northern Ontario, I prepared meals from a trailer, enjoying the shared comfort and community (excluding the bears) around a less-than-elegant dinner table. Later, my great friend Foofie and I started a catering company out of sheer will and resourcefulness, providing service to clients through what we came to know as entertaining.

Entertaining, to me, has never been synonymous with formality. Entertaining is simply hosting, taking care of people with some really good food and lots of drink. It can just as easily be on your back patio or a breakfast party in the kitchen with kids as it can be elegant cocktails or a formal sit-down with best friends or important clients. It's about creating an experience, one that regardless of size, scale or grandeur makes people smile and say, "That was a great party," without really knowing why.

When I opened dish, I was realizing my dream of creating a gathering place, a village where people could connect over good food through shared experiences. It is an expression of what I learned while working at *Toronto Life* magazine and from Peter Kump's Institute of Culinary Education (ICE) in New York. These places gave me the platform and the credibility to establish something different from a traditional restaurant (I lasted only 3 days in a New York restaurant kitchen!). My exposure to European approaches to food and wine, through my job with the travel company Butterfield & Robinson, was intoxicating (literally!) and fed my desire for a fresh take on dining, one that captured the magic of the bistros and vineyards of France.

And so I created **dish**, a cooking school and catering company that doubles as a cool venue for parties. The intent was to provide a fun and indulgent learning atmosphere with great food and wine. Our café and retail space give people a place to come day in, day out, for our homemade soups, sandwiches and dish-to-go prepared foods. The companion television show, *party dish*, was born out of the same desire to share experiences through creative themes, playful menus, shopping tips and innovative ways to entertain (like being a guest at your own party). This book is a culmination of that journey.

Good food helps bring balance to our busy lives by forcing us to sit, if only for a few minutes. My family will always be the great equalizer, keeping priorities straight—shared meals and a bit of downtime. My dad's growing vegetable garden and vineyard project, along with the Riverdale farmers' market at the end of the street will be a continued source of energy and passion, helping to keep the business of food focused on the food itself.

Most chapters of *dish entertains* are divided into two parts: Everyday Simple and Special Occasions. Everyday Simple is for your mid-week entertaining needs. (And remember, entertaining can even take the form of a meal at the kitchen counter with your spouse.) Special Occasions recipes are equally accessible but require a bit more time and effort. All the recipes in this book are meant to serve as platforms from which you can adjust, embellish or twist to suit your tastes, budget and lifestyle. I never was very good at following instructions, so I encourage you to take creative liberties!

Enjoy this book. Use it, share it and throw parties, planned or spur-of-the-moment. Entertain and gather around food in whatever style makes you happy. Just make sure it allows you to join the celebration, be it big, small, impromptu or one of life's milestones.

Enjoy! Trish

hors d'oeuvres

When we think of entertaining, we usually think of hors d'oeuvres—essential at celebratory, catered special events. Certainly hors d'oeuvres are the backbone of our catering business, but you can also do them yourself with these straightforward recipes. They may be a bit time consuming, but once you get rolling, you can be pretty efficient (think assembly line). The payoff is big—make ahead, feed a crowd, easy clean up and simple, beautiful presentation that will seriously impress your guests.

Delicious bite-and-a-half morsels are packed with flavour and beautifully presented. Here are my favourite (and our clients' favourite) hors d'oeuvres recipes, from catering, *party dish* and my own collection, with tips and secrets revealed in addition to the valuable input from our recipe testers and catering chefs who perfected them for home cooks. Enjoy the simple presentation ideas, fun twists, classic and new combinations.

As the seasons change, styles and palates change too, and we are constantly on a quest for new, delicious, fresh combinations and presentations. But as you'll see from these recipes, you just can't beat some of the classic matches like blue cheese with figs or smoked salmon with cream cheese. As with many things, the best recipes withstand the test of time.

It's also great to have a selection of dips, bar munchies and platters in your recipe arsenal for casual cocktail get-togethers. Stock up the fridge with interesting cheeses like Mimolette and Pierre Robert and the pantry with roasted red peppers, sun-dried tomatoes, balsamic vinegar, garlic, shallots and olive oil and you're on your way.

Have fun with the presentation—it's amazing what little vessels like tapas plates, shot glasses, espresso cups, petite dip bowls, a variety of white platters and some fun napkins and skewers can do. Stock your entertaining supply cupboard and you'll look like a pro at every gathering!

cocktail party guidelines

Follow these easy guidelines and you'll never need to worry again about the nuts and bolts of giving a cocktail party.

hors d'oeuvres portions

Pre-dinner: 3 pieces per person

Pre-dinner plus: 6 pieces per person (guests are not invited to stay over the dinner hour, but may be asked to join you at a restaurant afterwards)

Full cocktail party: 8 to 10 pieces per person plus a few substantial platters (in lieu of dinner, over the dinner hour)

rentals: to use or not to use

Inexpensive glassware is widely available (but ask yourself what your cleanup threshold is). Store extra party glasses in their boxes in the basement. For bigger parties, rent glasses so you can enjoy the party too.

Definitely invest in some inexpensive large square platters, some interesting low bowls and a few other mid-size white platters (they are pricey to rent). You'll use them to dress up your everyday meals too.

Door-to-door rental means drop-off of clean dishes and pickup of dirty (need I say more?). These are essential with groups over 12.

Linens: you'll have to launder or dry clean them anyway. Let the rental company handle it.

staffing

1 bartender for every 50 or so guests (unless you are getting into martinis and fancy concoctions)

1 to 2 wait staff for every 50 or so guests (depending on layout of space and formality of the function). Remember, they handle the cleanup!

1 to 2 kitchen staff for cocktails for 50, depending on the menu

EVERYDAY SIMPLE

---

asparagus wrapped with crispy pancetta and parmesan

smoked salmon bread sticks with caper cream cheese

roasted new potatoes with stilton cream and walnuts

cremini mushrooms stuffed with chèvre and leeks

figs with blue cheese and walnuts

fig, arugula and prosciutto rolls

yukon gold fries with spicy ketchup

easy smoked trout and avocado

asparagus wrapped with crispy pancetta and parmesan

The arrival of spring means asparagus for breakfast, lunch and dinner.
MAKES 20 HORS D'OEUVRES

INGREDIENTS
20 spears asparagus
1/2 to 2/3 cup (125 to 150 mL) freshly grated Parmesan cheese
Freshly ground pepper, to taste
10 slices pancetta (about 5 oz/150 g), cut in half

METHOD
Preheat oven to 450°F (230°C). Trim the woody ends off the asparagus spears and discard. Stir together Parmesan and pepper. Lay out each strip of pancetta and top with a row of Parmesan mixture across the bottom third. Place an asparagus spear on top of the cheese and roll up pancetta so that the asparagus ends are poking out on each side.

Place wrapped asparagus seam side down on a nonstick baking sheet (or a baking sheet lined with parchment paper). Bake for about 10 minutes, until asparagus is just cooked through and pancetta is crisp. Let cool slightly before serving, as these retain lots of heat!

These can be assembled (but not baked) up to 2 days ahead. Store in the fridge. Bake as directed when ready to serve. You can substitute prosciutto (shown here) or Parma ham for pancetta. Serve a few of the wrapped asparagus on top of dressed arugula or watercress to make a quick and elegant green salad. Or pop them under the broiler on jumbo crostini with a little extra cheese for a light dinner.

smoked salmon bread sticks with caper cream cheese

This is the quintessential pantry-essential hors d'oeuvre. Keep your pantry stocked with bread sticks and your fridge armed with capers, lemons, cream cheese and smoked salmon, and this will become your go-to-in-a-pinch nibble. When my sister-in-law Amanda tested this recipe, I arrived on the scene to find some enormous sticks with mounds of caper cream cheese and an entire piece of smoked salmon. We had a good laugh at the vague direction I had given on sizing. To keep things elegant, use small sticks, a little dab of cream cheese and a delicate amount of salmon.

MAKES 20 HORS D'OEUVRES

The Caper Cream Cheese can be made up to 2 days ahead and kept, covered, in the fridge. This hors d'oeuvre is best assembled just before serving to avoid soggy breadsticks.

Thin, elegant breadsticks are a great pantry staple. At dish, we serve soups in little espresso cups for a distinctive hors d'oeuvre. Just snap a breadstick in half and use it to garnish the little sips.

For a variation, spread some mascarpone cheese onto the breadstick and wrap with some thinly sliced prosciutto.

INGREDIENTS

Caper Cream Cheese

4 oz (125 g) cream cheese, softened
1/4 cup (50 mL) capers, drained
1/4 cup (50 mL) finely diced red onion
2 tbsp (25 mL) lemon zest
Salt and pepper, to taste

20 good-quality very thin bread sticks
10 to 15 slices smoked salmon, cut in half lengthwise

METHOD

In a food processor, pulse cream cheese, capers, onion and lemon zest until combined. Season with salt and pepper to taste.

Shortly before serving, spread about 1 tsp (5 mL) cream cheese mixture on bottom quarter of each breadstick. Wrap a strip of smoked salmon around cream cheese.

roasted new potatoes
with stilton cream and walnuts

This hors d'oeuvre has made a bit of a comeback. My friend Bay
tested this dish, and the hollowing out seemed to take some time—
I suggest getting a friend or spouse to pitch in to speed things up.
MAKES 20 HORS D'OEUVRES

To add an extra flavour dimension,
caramelize the walnuts. Here's a
quick method: toss the walnuts
with 1/4 cup (50 mL) brown sugar
and a pinch of salt. Spread out on a
parchment-lined baking sheet and
bake in a 350°F (180°C) oven for 12
minutes. Let cool.

INGREDIENTS

20 baby red new potatoes
1/4 cup (50 mL) olive oil
Salt and pepper, to taste
7 oz (200 g) Stilton, crumbled
1/2 cup (125 mL) cream cheese, softened
3 tbsp (50 mL) 35% cream
20 walnut halves, lightly toasted

METHOD

Preheat oven to 425°F (220°C). Trim a sliver off the bottom and top of each potato
(this will create a stable base for the halves to stand on), then cut in half horizon-
tally. Using a melon baller or a small spoon, carefully hollow out a bowl in each
potato half. Toss potatoes with oil and a good amount of salt and pepper. Place
potato halves on a baking sheet with the hollowed side down. Roast until they are
golden and tender, 20 to 30 minutes. Let cool.

In a medium bowl, use a fork to mix together Stilton, cream cheese and cream. Season with salt and pepper. Spoon a generous teaspoon (5 mL) of Stilton cream into
each hollowed potato. Top with a walnut half.

To serve: Preheat oven to 425°F (220°C). Stand stuffed potatoes on a baking sheet.
Bake until Stilton cream has just started to melt and potatoes are heated through,
6 to 8 minutes.

These hors d'oeuvres can be prepared up to 2 days ahead. Roast the potatoes

and stuff with the cheese mixture, then store, covered, in the refrigerator.

Let come to room temperature before baking.

cremini mushrooms stuffed with chèvre and leeks

This is not only make-ahead but travels well in a pizza box and impresses potluck party guests. MAKES 20 HORS D'OEUVRES

This flavour combination is perfect for a last-minute mid-week pasta dish. Cook your favourite pasta, sauté the leeks and sliced cremini mushrooms, then deglaze with some white wine. Toss the leeks and mush-rooms with the cooked pasta and add crumbled chèvre, a touch of good olive oil, sea salt and freshly ground black pepper. Easy and delicious!

Chefs and bakers always use unsalted butter and adjust the salt in a recipe themselves. If you're using salted butter, remember to reduce the amount of salt called for in the recipe. If unsalted butter really matters in a recipe in this book—such as in baked des-serts—the recipe will call for it.

The mushrooms can be assembled, but not baked, up to 1 day ahead. Cover and refrigerate. Bake as directed.

INGREDIENTS
4 1/2 oz (140 g) chèvre
Salt and pepper, to taste
20 large cremini mushrooms, stems removed, wiped clean
1 small leek (*white and light green part only*)
1 tbsp (15 mL) butter

METHOD
Preheat oven to 425°F (220°C). Line a baking sheet with parchment paper.

In a small bowl, mix together chèvre with salt and pepper. Fill centre of each mush-room cap with about 1 tbsp (15 mL) cheese mixture. Transfer to the baking sheet.

Cut leeks into 2-inch (5 cm) lengths, and slice each piece into very thin strips. Melt butter in a medium sauté pan over medium-high heat. Add leeks and cook for 1 to 2 minutes or until fragrant and translucent but not browned. Stir in a pinch of salt.

Top each stuffed mushroom with a pinch of the sautéed leeks. Bake mushrooms until cheese is just bubbly and mushrooms are tender, 7 to 10 minutes. Serve warm.

figs with blue cheese and walnuts

For our *party dish* stagette episode, we developed "emergency" hors d'oeuvres that were impressive and elegant and could be whipped up with guests already on your doorstep, still leaving you calm, cool and unflappable. Andrea and I still lean on this one in classes.

MAKES 20 HORS D'OEUVRES

Serve figs warm on crostini or on top of your favourite green salad. Use Gorgonzola or chèvre in place of Stilton. Use pecans or hazelnuts in place of walnuts.

INGREDIENTS

20 walnut halves
10 fresh figs
1/4 lb (125 g) good-quality blue cheese or Stilton
Salt and pepper, to taste
3 tbsp (50 mL) honey

METHOD

Preheat oven to 375°F (190°C). Lightly toast walnut halves on a baking sheet until fragrant (about 5 minutes).

Cut each fig in half, then cut a small slice off the side of each half so it will lie flat, cut side up. Arrange figs cut side up on the baking sheet. Top each fig half with a piece of blue cheese and a walnut half. Season with salt and pepper.

Bake for 5 minutes or until cheese is melted. Immediately drizzle each fig with a little honey and serve warm.

fig, arugula and prosciutto rolls

This is definitely a favourite dish hors d'oeuvre, surviving on our catering menu for years. It's simple yet elegant and is so beautiful on the plate.
MAKES 20 HORS D'OEUVRES

These can be made a few hours in advance. Store in an airtight container in the refrigerator.

This is a winning flavour combination. Turn into a delicious composed salad by dressing arugula with good olive oil and balsamic vinegar and top with fresh fig halves, some strips of prosciutto and some shaved Parmesan.

Use caramelized pear slices instead of figs. To caramelize pears, cut 3 pears into 8 slices each (cut out the core) and sauté in 2 tbsp (25 mL) butter on medium-high heat for a few minutes. Add 1 tbsp (15 mL) sugar and cook a bit longer, until sugar has melted and pears are golden.

INGREDIENTS
1/2 cup (125 mL) mascarpone cheese
Zest of 1 lemon
Salt and freshly ground pepper, to taste
10 slices prosciutto, cut slightly thicker than usual *(ask your butcher)*
1 bunch arugula, washed and dried, stems trimmed
6 fresh figs, sliced lengthwise *(you will need 20 full slices)*

METHOD
Stir together mascarpone cheese, lemon zest, salt and pepper until smooth.

Spread a thin layer of mascarpone mixture on the bottom third of each slice of prosciutto. Top cheese mixture with a few leaves of arugula; be sure to have the nicest part of the leaves poking out of both sides of the prosciutto. Lay 2 fig slices on top of the arugula and then roll up the prosciutto. Carefully cut the prosciutto rolls in half and stand up on a serving plate.

yukon gold fries with spicy ketchup

Everything old becomes new again. The hottest Toronto and New York restaurants popularized fries on their menus, calling up childhood memories of the old fry truck or fish-and-chips joint. All you need are little white paper cups and the kids (and the kid in you) are happy as can be.

MAKES ABOUT 20 PAPER CONES

Spicy Ketchup can be made up to a week ahead and stored in the fridge. Fries can be baked the day before, then re-crisped in a 450°F (230°C) oven for 5 to 10 minutes before serving. Leave some space between fries or they will be soggy. For an easy variation, use sweet potatoes instead.

Chipotle peppers are simply smoked jalapeños. You can find canned chipotles in most grocery stores. They come packed in adobo sauce, which you can add to the spicy ketchup to increase the heat factor. If you can't find chipotles, you can spice up your ketchup with cayenne pepper, dried chili flakes or your favourite hot sauce. One chipotle goes a long way. Some other uses are our Sweet Potato Chipotle Soup (page 86) or any other soup, or in a wet marinade for chicken and ribs.

An ode to Quebec: replace the spicy ketchup with mayonnaise.

INGREDIENTS

6 medium Yukon Gold potatoes, unpeeled
1/4 cup (50 mL) extra-virgin olive oil
Kosher salt and pepper, to taste
Maldon sea salt
Fresh thyme, finely chopped

Spicy Ketchup
1 cup (250 mL) ketchup
1 chipotle pepper, finely minced

METHOD

Preheat oven to 425°F (220°C). Cut each potato into wedges about 3 inches (8 cm) long and 3/4 inch (2 cm) wide. In a bowl, toss fries with olive oil; season with salt and pepper and toss again to coat. Lay fries out on a baking sheet, leaving a bit of space in between each one. Bake fries for 30 to 40 minutes, turning once halfway through, until golden and crisp. Remove from oven and immediately toss with a little more kosher salt, some Maldon sea salt and fresh thyme.

In a small bowl, stir together ketchup and chipotle pepper.

TO SERVE

Family-style: Transfer warm fries to a platter and serve with bowl of spicy ketchup.

Individual hors d'oeuvres: Place a tablespoon or so (15 mL) of spicy ketchup in small paper cones or plain Dixie cups. Fill each cone with 5 or 6 fries.

easy smoked trout and avocado

I was introduced to smoked trout at my husband's family cottage on Georgian Bay, where a shop in Lafontaine brings in its daily catch and smokes it on site. Pam, my school director, and I rank it our No. 1 summer favourite. MAKES 24 HORS D'OEUVRES

The smoked trout can be flaked a day ahead. Pull it apart where it naturally breaks, and then cut into bite-size pieces. You can make the avocado purée a few hours ahead. To keep from oxidizing and turning brown, sprinkle with lime juice and press plastic wrap directly onto the surface.

If you want to get fancy (and if you have the time), whip up potato rösti or a rice pancake to replace the quickie cracker.

Smoked trout is a wonderful brunch option in place of smoked salmon. Serve with avocado, Caper Cream Cheese (page 22) and brown breads. Or serve à la niçoise, with cherry tomatoes, green beans and mayonnaise.

INGREDIENTS
1 ripe avocado
1 clove garlic, minced
1/2 medium jalapeño pepper, seeds and ribs removed, minced
2 tbsp (25 mL) minced red onion
Juice of 1 lime
Salt and pepper, to taste
20 rice crackers
1/2 side smoked trout, flaked into generous 1-inch (2 cm) pieces

METHOD
In a bowl, mash avocado flesh with a fork. Add the garlic, jalapeño, red onion, lime juice and a few good pinches of salt and pepper.
Spoon about 1 tbsp (15 mL) avocado purée onto each rice cracker.
Top with a piece of smoked trout and serve immediately.

SPECIAL OCCASIONS

———

crab cakes with lime aïoli

pistachio-dusted date and chèvre "truffles"

jumbo shrimp cocktail shooters

indian-spiced chicken skewers with cool raita

fresh thai salad rolls with sake-lime dip

lobster and citrus salad on endive

scallop ceviche with avocado

crab cakes with lime aïoli

This hors d'oeuvre is certainly a labour of love, but enjoy a Sunday afternoon in the kitchen, double your batch and freeze half for later.

MAKES 30 HORS D'OEUVRES

Some of the ingredients listed may be a little hard to find, but they are worth the effort! You can find lemongrass, lime leaves and sambal chili paste at your city's Asian markets, and many grocery stores now carry lemongrass and sambal. If you can't find them, don't worry! Your crab cakes will still be delicious.

Lime Aïoli can be made up to 3 days in advance. Refrigerate, covered. "Aïoli" just means homemade mayo with garlic. As you can see, we are using store-bought and dressing it up.

Crab Cakes

2 tbsp (25 mL) butter

1 tbsp (15 mL) grapeseed oil

1 tbsp (15 mL) minced fresh ginger

1 tbsp (15 mL) minced garlic

1 stalk lemongrass, woody outer layers removed, heart minced

4 green onions, finely chopped

1 shallot, minced

2 kaffir lime leaves, stems removed, minced

Salt and pepper, to taste

1 lb (500 g) best-quality claw crabmeat, drained and picked over

Juice of 1 lime

1/4 cup (50 mL) mayonnaise

1 to 3 tbsp (15 to 50 mL) sambal chili paste or hot sauce

3 large eggs

2 cups (500 mL) panko bread crumbs

1 cup (250 mL) all-purpose flour

Salt and pepper, to taste

1 to 2 cups (250 to 500 mL) vegetable oil, for frying

Lime Aïoli

1/4 cup (50 mL) mayonnaise

Zest of 1 lime

1 clove garlic, minced

METHOD

To make Lime Aïoli, in a bowl, combine mayonnaise, lime zest and garlic.

To make the crab cakes, in a large sauté pan over medium-high heat, heat butter and oil until foamy. Add ginger, garlic, lemongrass, green onions, shallot and lime leaves; sauté for 5 to 7 minutes, stirring often, until fragrant and light brown or golden. Season with salt and pepper. Let cool completely.

In a large bowl, combine sautéed mixture, crabmeat, lime juice and mayonnaise. Stir together and season to taste with chili paste, salt and pepper.

Using your hands, shape 1 1/2 tbsp (22 mL) crab mixture into a little puck. Place on a tray or plate that will fit in your freezer. Proceed with the rest of the mix. Place crab cakes in the freezer for 30 minutes to help set their shape.

In a shallow bowl, whisk together the eggs. Put panko and flour in two separate bowls. Season each bowl with a pinch of salt and pepper. Dip each crab cake into the flour just to coat. Next, dip into egg, letting the excess run off. Then coat each crab cake with panko. Return to the tray and freeze again for 20 minutes.

Heat a large sauté pan over medium heat. When it is hot, add 1/2 inch (1 cm) of oil. When oil is hot but not smoking, fry crab cakes in batches, turning once, until golden, about 3 minutes per side. Don't worry about heating them through, as you will be flashing them in the oven before serving. Drain crab cakes on paper towels. (Crab cakes can be fried a few hours ahead.)

When ready to serve, preheat oven to 425°F (220°C). Place crab cakes on a baking sheet and bake until just warmed through and re-crisped, 7 to 9 minutes. To serve, top with a small dollop of lime aïoli.

Crab cakes can be shaped and breaded, then frozen for up to 3 months, stored in an airtight container. Fry the crab cakes from frozen and bake for an additional 2 to 3 minutes.

Make 4 to 6 larger crab cakes. Add about 5 minutes to the baking time so they fully warm through. This is an elegant but comforting appetizer.

pistachio-dusted date and chèvre "truffles"

This is a fabulous hands-on, interactive hors d'oeuvre. Pour the wine and get the aprons on—these are messy! MAKES ABOUT 20 HORS D'OUEVRES

INGREDIENTS

4 oz (125 g) chèvre, softened
2 oz (60 g) cream cheese, softened
2 tbsp (25 mL) cassis or port
Salt and pepper, to taste
10 dates, pitted and halved crosswise
1/2 cup (125 mL) pistachios, lightly toasted and ground

METHOD

In a bowl, mix together chèvre and cream cheese with a fork. Add cassis and a pinch of salt; mix until smooth. Chill for 30 minutes.

Measure out about 1 tbsp (15 mL) chèvre mixture. Press a date half into mixture. Cover date and chèvre with plastic wrap. Use the plastic wrap to help you evenly distribute the cheese around the date to create a little ball with the date half inside. Remove plastic wrap. Continue with remaining mixture and dates.

Spread ground pistachios on a small plate. Season with a touch of salt and pepper. Roll each chèvre "truffle" in pistachios to coat evenly. Refrigerate, covered, until serving.

"Truffles" can be made up to 2 days in advance. Cover and refrigerate. Try using green grapes in place of the dates. You can also replace the pistachios with crushed toasted walnuts, pecans or hazelnuts.

Try out this flavour combination for a simple salad with impact: dress salad greens with a simple lemon vinaigrette. Scatter with pistachios, crumbled chèvre and dates or grapes.

These hors d'oeuvres are rich and should be made small. Think two wee bites, about the size of a chocolate truffle.

jumbo shrimp cocktail shooters

Through the years we have exchanged funky little sherry glasses for short shot glasses, and a curry sauce for a cocktail sauce. Change it up if you like: make the shrimp the same way but serve them with shooters of Green Gazpacho (page 90, pictured here) or a simple Thai green curry coconut sauce (green curry paste, fish sauce and coconut milk).

MAKES 20 HORS D'OEUVRES

Cocktail Sauce can be made up to 3 days in advance. Shrimp can be cooked earlier in the day and served cold.

INGREDIENTS

Shrimp and Marinade

20 shrimp *(16 to 20 per pound size)*, peeled, deveined, tail left on

1 tbsp (15 mL) sambal chili paste *(or 1 tsp/5 mL hot sauce)*

1 tbsp (15 mL) lemon zest

1 tbsp (15 mL) lime zest

2 cloves garlic, finely minced

1/4 cup (50 mL) grapeseed or canola oil

Salt and pepper, to taste

Cocktail Sauce

1 1/2 cups (375 mL) ketchup

1/2 cup (125 mL) chili sauce

2 cloves garlic, finely minced

1/3 cup (75 mL) finely grated fresh horseradish

2 tbsp (25 mL) lemon juice

2 tbsp (25 mL) lime juice

Tabasco sauce, to taste

Worcestershire sauce, to taste

Salt and pepper, to taste

METHOD

Combine shrimp with all the marinade ingredients. Let marinate for 30 minutes.

Combine all ingredients for the cocktail sauce and season to taste. Transfer to a large measuring cup or pitcher.

Preheat broiler to high. Spread out the marinated shrimp on a baking sheet and broil for 2 to 3 minutes, until they start to turn pink and curl up. Turn shrimp and broil for 1 more minute. Remove from heat immediately and let cool slightly.

To serve, carefully pour cocktail sauce into shot glasses. Perch a shrimp on the rim of each glass and serve.

indian-spiced chicken skewers with cool raita

This recipe is a labour of love, but every bite will tell you it was worth it! Little boats are a fun presentation and keep the party clothes stain-free.

MAKES 20 HORS D'OEUVRES

When making the skewers, be sure not to poke the point of the skewer through the top of the chicken. Skewers look best with the wooden tip hidden.

Chicken skewers can be fully assembled, but not broiled, up to 1 day ahead. Store covered in the refrigerator. Raita can be made earlier in the day and kept refrigerated.

Give each guest several chicken skewers and serve with some fragrant basmati rice, warm naan bread and a baby spinach salad for an easy Indian-spiced meal.

You can also try Thai-inspired flavours here: for the marinade, use 1 cup (250 mL) coconut milk, 3 tbsp (50 mL) fish sauce, 1 tsp (5 mL) Thai curry paste, the juice and zest of a lime and 1 tbsp (15 mL) sugar. Serve with Peanut Sauce (page 151).

INGREDIENTS

Chicken and Marinade

3 cloves garlic
1 tbsp (15 mL) minced fresh ginger
3 tbsp (50 mL) lemon juice
1 cup (250 mL) plain yogurt
3 tbsp (50 mL) of your favourite curry powder, curry paste or tandoori paste
2 tbsp (25 mL) salt
1 pinch saffron threads, crumbled (*optional*)
2 lb (1 kg) boneless skinless chicken breast, trimmed of fat

Raita

1/2 medium English cucumber, unpeeled
2 cups (500 mL) 3.2% plain yogurt
2 cloves garlic, minced
1 tbsp (15 mL) finely chopped fresh cilantro
Juice of 1 lime
Salt and pepper, to taste

METHOD

In a food processor, process garlic, ginger, lemon juice and yogurt until smooth. Add curry powder, salt and saffron; pulse to combine. Set 1/2 cup (125 mL) aside for basting.

Slice chicken into 20 strips 3 inches (8 cm) long, 1 inch (2.5 cm) wide and 1 inch (2.5 cm) thick. Place strips in a resealable plastic bag and pour in rest of marinade. Marinate, refrigerated, at least 4 hours and preferably overnight.

Coarsely grate the cucumber. Place cucumber inside a clean tea towel and twist it hard to squeeze out as much liquid as possible. In a bowl, combine cucumber with yogurt, garlic, cilantro and lime juice. Season with salt and pepper.

Preheat broiler to high. Line a baking sheet with foil. Thread marinated chicken onto 6-inch (15 cm) wooden skewers (*see tip*). Use a strip of foil to cover the exposed wooden skewers (to prevent burning). Season chicken with salt and pepper and brush with some of the reserved marinade. Broil chicken for 3 to 5 minutes per side, brushing again when you flip skewers, until no longer pink inside.

Serve hot chicken skewers with raita.

fresh thai salad rolls with sake-lime dip

If you aren't quick with a knife, use your food processor. Use the julienne attachment to get perfect thin strips of cucumbers, peppers and carrots.

MAKES 20 HORS D'OEUVRES

Sake-Lime Dip can be made 1 day ahead. Rolls can be assembled up to 4 hours ahead. Keep them covered with a damp cloth and plastic wrap and refrigerate. You can get as creative as you want with the ingredients for these rolls—jicama, avocado, green mango, bean sprouts, orange peppers, green apple—the list is endless!

For a more substantial starter, cut rolls in half and serve as a plated appetizer.

Purchase sake in the liquor store near the fortified wines.

INGREDIENTS

Sake-Lime Dip

1/4 cup (50 mL) sake or mirin
1/4 cup (50 mL) lime juice
1 tsp (5 mL) sambal oelek chili paste
3 tbsp (50 mL) finely chopped green onion
2 tbsp (25 mL) sugar
2 tbsp (25 mL) grapeseed or canola oil
Kosher salt, to taste

Rolls

1 lb (500 g) rice stick (vermicelli) noodles
Leaves from 1/2 bunch Thai basil
1 medium carrot, peeled and julienned
1 mango, peeled and julienned
1 red bell pepper, julienned
1/2 English cucumber, peeled and julienned
1/2 cup (125 mL) cashews, toasted and crushed
10 (10-inch/25 cm) rice paper wrappers

METHOD

To make the Sake-Lime Dip, in a bowl, whisk together sake, lime juice, chili paste, green onion and sugar. Slowly whisk in oil until dip emulsifies. Season with salt and set aside.

Soak noodles in hot water until tender (about 10 minutes). Drain.

Meanwhile, prepare the vegetables and set up an "assembly line" with all the Thai roll ingredients laid out. Place a clean tea towel on your work surface.

Fill a shallow pan with hot water. Soak 1 rice paper wrapper in the hot water until soft and pliable (about 30 seconds). Place the rice paper wrapper on the tea towel and pat dry. Along the bottom third of the wrapper, place a small amount of noodles, Thai basil, julienned vegetables and cashews. Keeping the rice paper taut, fold ends in first, then tightly roll up into a cigar shape.

Soak and pat dry another rice paper wrapper and wrap it around the Thai roll. This will give the roll strength and make it easier to cut. Cover roll with a damp towel. Make more rolls with the remaining ingredients. Keep them covered with the damp towel.

Cut each roll in 4 or 5 small pieces using a very sharp knife. Serve with Sake-Lime Dip.

lobster and citrus salad on endive

We did a version of this on *party dish*. We filmed a lobster-shopping segment at Bill's Lobster on Gerrard St. in Toronto. After we had selected the perfect canners (small 3/4-lb lobsters), Bill pointed at his freezer stocked with flash-frozen lobster meat and suggested I could save a lot of time by buying frozen meat, especially for bite-size portions—a shortcut worth taking! MAKES 20 HORS D'OEUVRES

The citrus sections, lobster and vinaigrette can be prepared up to a day ahead. Store them separately in the fridge. Bring to room temperature and toss together shortly before using.

Use cooked shrimp in place of the lobster meat for an easier and less expensive hors d'oeuvre.

Serve some of the lobster-citrus salad on a bed of Belgian endive and Boston lettuce for a fresh, light lunch.

INGREDIENTS

6 oz (175 g) cooked lobster meat, fresh, frozen or
    good-quality canned *(the meat from a 1 1/4-lb/625 g lobster)*
2 navel oranges
1 small red grapefruit
1/2 shallot, finely minced
3 tbsp (50 mL) grapeseed oil
Salt and pepper, to taste
20 Belgian endive leaves

METHOD

Chop lobster meat into 1/4-inch (0.5 cm) pieces. Place in a large bowl.

Using a sharp knife, remove all peel and white pith from the oranges and grapefruit. Working over a bowl to catch the juices, use knife to slice out citrus sections from between the membranes. Cut citrus sections into 1/4-inch (0.5 cm) pieces and add to lobster. Set aside juices.

In a small bowl, whisk 2 tbsp (25 mL) reserved citrus juice with shallot, grapeseed oil and salt and pepper until emulsified. Add to lobster. Season with salt and pepper and toss well.

Using a small, sharp knife, shave a small piece off the back of each endive leaf (this will form a base so it will stay upright on the plate). Right before serving, place a heaping teaspoonful of lobster salad at the bottom end of each endive spear.

scallop ceviche with avocado

"Ceviche" simply means raw fish marinated in citrus juice. The acid in the juice "cooks" the fish, firming it and turning it opaque.
MAKES ABOUT 20 HORS D'OEUVRES

The scallops can be marinated, covered and refrigerated, up to 6 hours ahead. Combine scallops with the rest of the ingredients closer to serving time.

Try using other types of white fish for this ceviche (Pacific halibut, tilapia, striped bass and Pacific sole work well). Slice thinly or dice into small cubes. Anytime you are making ceviche, it is imperative to obtain the freshest fish and seafood you can possibly find, preferably bought on the day you are serving it.

Andrea and I were both pregnant when developing this dish. The thought of ceviche made us nervous, so we lightly poached the scallops in boiling water for 30 seconds, then drained them and patted them dry before mixing them with the citrus juices.

INGREDIENTS

3/4 lb (375 g) fresh medium sea scallops, muscle removed
1/4 cup (50 mL) fresh lime juice
2 or 3 oranges, blood oranges or red grapefruits
2 tbsp (25 mL) finely minced red onion
1 tbsp (15 mL) finely minced seeded jalapeño pepper
1/2 avocado, cut into 1/2-inch (1 cm) cubes
Maldon sea salt, to taste
Extra-virgin olive oil, to taste

METHOD

Lay the scallops on their sides and, using a very sharp knife, cut each scallop crosswise into 3 or 4 slices about 1/4-inch (0.5 cm) thick. In a nonaluminum bowl, mix scallop slices with the lime juice, coating well, and refrigerate while you prepare the other citrus.

Using a sharp knife, remove all peel and white pith from citrus fruits. Working over a bowl to catch the juices, use knife to slice out citrus sections from between the membranes. Set aside juices. Cut citrus sections into 1/4-inch (0.5 cm) pieces. Set aside.

Add reserved citrus juices to scallops; mix well and refrigerate for at least 30 minutes but no more than 6 hours. The acid in the citrus juice will "cook" the scallops, and when ready, the scallops will be opaque.

Before serving, add red onion, citrus sections, jalapeño and avocado to the scallops. Season well with Maldon sea salt and add a dash of extra-virgin olive oil. Gently stir together just to combine.

There are many vessels for serving this hors d'oeuvre. Some of our favourites are little white ceramic wonton spoons, chilled shot glasses with fun toothpicks or tiny soy sauce bowls that you can find in Asian markets. Or, for a more organic base, try serving a heaping tablespoon of scallop ceviche on the inner leaves of Boston lettuce (or more, as a fantastic salad).

NIBBLES

═══

the cheese table

sourdough rosemary boule

crostini

sweet pea mash

roasted red pepper dip

zesty mini pita crisps

sun-dried tomato and feta dip

hot cheese dip

tuscan bean dip

mango salsa

curry dip

classic buttermilk chive dip

baked olives with orange and oregano

spiced nuts

savoury baked brie

platters, bars & stations

the cheese table

In the past few years, cheese has become more popular than ever, with so many Canadian cheeses available from top-notch producers. When buying cheese, plan on about 2 to 4 oz (60 to 125 g) total per person, but make sure you have a few different varieties on hand. A good general rule is to have one soft, creamy cheese, one tangy, fresh chèvre, one hard, dry cheese and one blue or veiny cheese. Ask your cheesemonger for help, introductions to new ideas and, of course, for tasters! Alex Farms and The Cheese Boutique in Toronto inspire me with new tastes every time.

More than four varieties on one platter tends to be overkill. If you serve the cheeses on individual plates, lay them out from mildest to strongest, label them with little cards and suggest your guests try them in that order. Make sure to inform your guests which cheeses are unpasteurized.

HARD, DRY CHEESES
Manchego
Comte
Aged Cheddar
Emmental
Mimolette
Pecorino Romano and Toscano

CHÈVRES
Valençay
Chèvre d'Or

SOFT TRIPLE CREAMS
Reblochon
Délice de Bourgogne
Pierre Robert
Brie Supreme
Brie de Meaux

VEINY BLUE CHEESES
Roaring Forties
Gorgonzola
Stilton
Morbier

SIMPLE ACCOMPANIMENTS
Fresh fruits
   Concord grapes, pears (Bosc, Bartlett, Forelle, Anjou), Granny Smith apples, figs, blackberries, raspberries, kumquats, apricots, plums, prune plums
Dried fruits
   Medjool dates, figs, apricots, cranberries, prunes, mangoes
Toasted nuts
   walnuts, pecans, whole almonds
Breads
   Mix up size, shape and flavour; go rustic and different with olive or raisin walnut boule, ficelle, cracker breads

For a casual gathering, think "French picnic" and go for a rustic cheese table with burlap and natural fabrics. Lay cheeses out on food-safe slate, marble or old wooden cutting boards. Fruit and sliced breads look great straight on the table or in baskets. Leave the cheeses in big hunks with dedicated cheese knives nearby for your guests to pick away with. For a more formal gathering, create beautiful cheese plates or platters for an after-dinner treat. Make sure to pull the cheeses out of the fridge at least 30 minutes before serving—cheese is best at room temperature. Cheese is intended to be eaten on its own or with simple accompaniments.

sourdough rosemary boule

This is the simplest nibble ever. Putting store-bought bread into the oven for a few minutes is one of my favourite entertaining tricks—it fills the air with the smell of fresh-baked bread. This works with frozen bread or to freshen up day-old bread (works in real estate too if you are trying to sell your home!). Serve with olives, cheese, any of our dips or just good olive oil and balsamic vinegar in a dish for dipping. SERVES 6

INGREDIENTS

1 large sourdough boule (about 12 oz/375 g)
1/4 cup (50 mL) olive oil
1 tbsp (15 mL) chopped fresh rosemary
Flaky sea salt, to taste

METHOD

Preheat oven to 350°F (180°C). Cut boule into 10 slices, each 1 inch (2 cm) thick, stopping halfway down and keeping boule intact. Drizzle olive oil and sprinkle rosemary and salt down between the slices and on top of the bread. Wrap boule in foil. Place on a baking sheet and bake for 20 minutes or until warm and crunchy.

crostini

Crostini when in Italy, croûtes when in France. Crostini are the perfect quick, inexpensive base to create an endless variety of nibbles from casual to elegant. They are also perfect to accompany a salad or soup or as a light lunch on their own. Simply toast baguette or other bread slices in a 350°F (180°C) oven until they are golden and firm, 10 minutes. Drizzle a bit of olive oil and sprinkle some salt on them before baking. Here are some great topping ideas to get you started.

Crostini can be made up to 2 days ahead. Store in an airtight container at room temperature. If they get stale, simply re-crisp them in the oven for a few minutes.

Mushroom duxelles (sautéed mushrooms with cream, reduced till thickened)

Comte or old Cheddar and sliced apple

Mascarpone, arugula and fresh fig

Ricotta, watercress and caramelized pear

Sweet Pea Mash (opposite) with shaved pecorino or Parmesan cheese

Soft mozzarella *(bocconcini)*, pesto and cherry tomatoes

Latin-spiced Beef with Smoky Tomato Relish (page 162)

Brie, apple slices and candied walnuts

Chèvre, sautéed leeks and pine nuts

Slow-roasted Tomatoes (page 189), mozzarella and tapenade

Caper Cream Cheese (page 22) and smoked salmon

Parmesan, prosciutto, fig and balsamic reduction

Roast turkey, homemade cranberry sauce and Brie

Thinly sliced grilled chicken breast with pesto and Slow-roasted Tomatoes (page 189)

sweet pea mash

I love this dip's vibrant green colour. It starts to fade after a day in the fridge, so the dip is best blended the day of, although you can roast the garlic and blanch the peas a day before. This was inspired by my San Francisco cooking school mentor, Mary Risley (Tante Marie), who had us make a fava bean mash in the spring—lots of shucking and peeling, so I substituted peas. MAKES ABOUT 2 CUPS (500 ML)

INGREDIENTS

2 cups (500 mL) frozen peas, preferably baby peas or petits pois,
   or fresh peas when in season
1/2 small shallot
1 head garlic, roasted *(see tip)*
Zest and juice of 1 small lemon
6 tbsp (90 mL) good-quality olive oil
1/2 cup (125 mL) finely grated Parmesan cheese
Salt and pepper, to taste

METHOD

To blanch the peas, bring a medium pot of salted water to a boil. Get a bowl of ice water ready. Cook the peas in the boiling water for 1 to 2 minutes or until bright green and just tender. Drain the peas and immediately immerse in the ice water to stop the cooking. When cool, drain and lay flat on paper towels to dry.

In a food processor, pulse shallot and roasted garlic until finely chopped. Add the blanched peas and lemon zest and juice; pulse again until smooth. With machine running, drizzle olive oil through feed tube.

Once combined, stir in Parmesan cheese and season with salt and pepper.

TO ROAST GARLIC: Using a sharp knife, slice off the top of an unpeeled head of garlic, just enough to expose the tops of the cloves. Drizzle with 1 tablespoon (15 mL) olive oil and wrap loosely in foil. Transfer to a baking sheet and bake at 425°F (220°C) until garlic is tender (about 45 minutes). When cool, squeeze roasted garlic out of skins.

Turn this dip into a quick-and-easy hors d'oeuvre by spreading it on pieces of crostini and topping with a curl of Parmesan or pecorino cheese. It also looks great as part of a trio of dips with assorted breads. Garnish with a drizzle of good olive oil.

roasted red pepper dip

This is a quick make-ahead dip, perfect with crudités or our Zesty Mini Pita Crisps. It's also great tossed in pasta as your base sauce.
MAKES ABOUT 1 1/2 CUPS (375 ML)

INGREDIENTS

1 jar (500 mL) roasted red peppers, drained,
   rinsed and chopped
1 clove garlic
1 shallot, chopped
4 oz (125 g) soft chèvre
Kosher salt and freshly ground pepper, to taste

METHOD

In a food processor, combine red peppers, garlic
   and shallot. Process until smooth.
Add chèvre. Process until well combined. Season
   with salt and pepper.
Transfer to a serving bowl. Cover and refrigerate
   until serving.

zesty mini pita crisps

Here's a quick and healthy alternative to crackers. SERVES 4 TO 6 WITH DIP

INGREDIENTS

1 pkg mini pita rounds, white or whole wheat
   (see tip), whole or cut in half
2 tbsp (25 mL) olive oil
1/2 tsp (2 mL) kosher salt
1/4 tsp (1 mL) paprika
1/4 tsp (1 mL) cayenne pepper

METHOD

Preheat oven to 350°F (180°C). On a baking sheet, lay
   out mini pitas in a single layer. Brush with olive oil
   on both sides. In a small bowl, mix salt, paprika and
   cayenne pepper. Sprinkle evenly over pitas. Bake until
   crispy (about 10 minutes). Let cool. Store cooled crisps
   in an airtight container for up to 1 week.

You can also cut 4 large pitas into 6 wedges each, to yield 24
pieces. To keep pitas flat, bake with a second baking sheet
placed on top, sandwiching the pitas.

sun-dried tomato and feta dip

This popular dip can be made several days in advance, so it's perfect for casual entertaining. Try it as a spread for sandwiches (great for summer picnics) and even as a pesto-like sauce with pasta. We often serve this with little flatbreads and baked olives as a nibble before our cooking classes. MAKES ABOUT 3 CUPS (750 ML)

INGREDIENTS

2 cups (500 mL) drained oil-packed sun-dried tomatoes
2 cloves garlic
3/4 cup (175 mL) crumbled feta cheese
2 tbsp (25 mL) chopped fresh basil
2 tbsp (25 mL) balsamic vinegar
1 tsp (5 mL) dried chili flakes, or more to taste
4 to 6 tbsp (50 to 90 mL) olive oil
Salt and pepper, to taste

METHOD

Put the sun-dried tomatoes, garlic, feta, basil, vinegar and chili flakes in a
    food processor and pulse to a thick purée. Add 4 tbsp (50 mL) oil and pulse
    to combine. Pulse in up to 2 tbsp (25 mL) more oil until desired consistency is
    reached. Stir in salt and pepper.
Serve on toasted baguette slices or any nice bread you have on hand.

hot cheese dip

Cool weather calls for warm-up-the-belly nibbles. Pace yourself—once you start, it's hard to stop! Serve with crackers. MAKES ABOUT 2 CUPS (500 ML)

INGREDIENTS
1 cup (250 mL) grated white Cheddar cheese
1 cup (250 mL) mayonnaise
1/2 cup (125 mL) finely chopped green onion
1 tsp (5 mL) dry mustard
1 tsp (5 mL) Worcestershire sauce
1/2 tsp (2 mL) cayenne pepper
1/2 tsp (2 mL) Tabasco sauce
Salt and pepper, to taste

METHOD
Preheat oven to 350°F (180°C).

In a bowl, combine all ingredients and stir together well. Place in a small oven-to-table dish and bake for 30 minutes or until browning and bubbly.

To serve, wrap the hot dish in a pretty tea towel, place it on a rustic breadboard and surround with crackers.

tuscan bean dip

A simple, flavourful pantry-essential dip, easy to have on hand and healthy, too.
MAKES 1 1/2 CUPS (375 ML)

INGREDIENTS
1/4 cup (50 mL) extra-virgin olive oil
3 cloves garlic, crushed
1 can (19 oz/540 mL) cannellini or navy beans, drained and rinsed
3/4 tsp (4 mL) chopped fresh rosemary
Kosher salt and freshly ground pepper, to taste

METHOD
Heat olive oil in a small sauté pan over medium-low heat. Add crushed garlic and simmer gently until fragrant and soft (about 5 minutes). Let cool slightly. Remove garlic with a slotted spoon and let oil cool.

In a food processor, combine beans and garlic. Process until smooth. With machine running, drizzle cooled olive oil through feed tube until well blended. Add rosemary, salt and pepper. Pulse until blended.

Transfer to a serving bowl. Garnish with a few rosemary leaves and a drizzle of olive oil, if desired.

mango salsa

This salsa is the perfect summer accompaniment to grilled fish or chicken. In our university days, my friend Kristi and I used this to dress simple grilled dinners. Try adding papaya with the mango. If you're using this as a dip, serve with tortilla chips. MAKES ABOUT 3 CUPS (750 ML)

INGREDIENTS
2 slightly under-ripe mangoes, peeled and diced
1/2 cup (125 mL) diced red onion
1/2 cup (125 mL) finely chopped fresh basil
1 jalapeño chili, seeds removed and minced
1 red bell pepper, diced
Zest of 1 lime
1/3 cup (75 mL) lime juice *(from 2 to 3 limes)*
4 tsp (20 mL) grapeseed or canola oil
Kosher salt and black pepper, to taste

METHOD
In a bowl, combine mango, red onion, basil, jalapeño and red pepper. Stir in lime zest and juice, oil, salt and pepper.
Let sit for 30 minutes for flavours to combine.

curry dip

There's something about recipes from the '70s that have staying power. Fat content? Just remember, everything in moderation—and I've lightened the mayo with a sour cream or yogurt alternative. This was my favourite dip when I was growing up—and my mom's clever way to get us to eat our veggies. MAKES 1 CUP (250 ML)

INGREDIENTS

1/2 cup (125 mL) light mayonnaise
1/2 cup (125 mL) sour cream or plain yogurt
3 tbsp (50 mL) chili sauce
2 tsp (10 mL) mild curry powder
1 tsp (5 mL) Worcestershire sauce
1/2 tsp (2 mL) onion powder
1/2 tsp (2 mL) seasoned salt

METHOD

In a bowl, mix together all ingredients until combined.
   Serve with crudités.

classic buttermilk chive dip

When it comes to dips, just about every one pairs well with crudités. MAKES 2 CUPS (500 ML)

INGREDIENTS

1 clove garlic, finely minced
1 1/2 cups (375 mL) plain yogurt or sour cream
1/4 cup (50 mL) mayonnaise
1/4 cup (50 mL) buttermilk
2 tbsp (25 mL) finely chopped fresh chives
1 tbsp (15 mL) fresh lemon juice
A dash each Worcestershire sauce and Tabasco sauce
Salt and pepper, to taste

METHOD

In a bowl, whisk together all ingredients until smooth.
   Serve with crudités.

baked olives with orange and oregano

Make these ahead and warm through in the oven on a baking sheet just before guests arrive. Or to make life even easier, simply serve at room temperature. These olives will keep for several days in the fridge.
SERVES 8

We are constantly experiment-
ing with different flavours in this
recipe. Try lemon/shallot/thyme,
blood orange/basil/chili, orange/
rosemary/fennel or anything else
you can think of! Just be sure to
use fresh herbs or the flavour
won't be as good.

INGREDIENTS
3 cups (750 mL) mixed olives *(kalamata, green, niçoise)*
1 unpeeled navel orange, sliced into medium rings
2 cloves garlic, finely minced
1 long red chili, thinly sliced *(or 2 tsp/10 mL dried chili flakes)*
2 tbsp (25 mL) roughly chopped fresh oregano
3 tbsp (50 mL) extra-virgin olive oil
Freshly ground pepper, to taste

METHOD
Preheat oven to 350°F (180°C). Place all the ingredients on a large baking sheet
    and toss thoroughly together. Place another baking sheet on top of the olives to
    press them down and keep all the flavours in. Bake until olives are warm and
    flavours are combined (about 20 minutes).
Serve warm or at room temperature.

spiced nuts

These nuts are a great nibble and can be made a week in advance and stored in an airtight container at room temperature. Try playing around with the spicing—smoked paprika and ground coriander or cardamom and cayenne. MAKES ABOUT 2 CUPS (500 ML)

INGREDIENTS

1/2 cup (125 mL) maple syrup or honey
2 tsp (10 mL) salt
1 tsp (5 mL) black pepper
1/4 tsp (1 mL) ground allspice
1/4 tsp (1 mL) cayenne pepper
2 cups (500 mL) mixed unsalted nuts *(almonds, pecans, walnuts, hazelnuts, pepitas)*
2 tbsp (25 mL) sugar

METHOD

Preheat oven to 350°F (180°C). Line a baking sheet with parchment paper.

Stir together maple syrup, salt, black pepper, allspice and cayenne. Add nuts and toss to coat well. Lay coated nuts on the baking sheet, spreading them out as much as possible so they don't stick together too much. Bake for 10 minutes.

Sprinkle sugar over the nuts and give them a stir. Return nuts to the oven and bake for about 5 more minutes, until fragrant and medium brown and sugar and spices adhere together. Let nuts cool on the baking sheet. When nuts are cool, break them apart if needed, and serve.

savoury baked brie

Baked Brie is a classic party dish—a warm, melting round of cheese with a savoury, crunchy topping. SERVES 10 TO 12

INGREDIENTS

3 cups (750 mL) arugula, stems removed

1/4 cup (50 mL) lightly toasted pine nuts

4 tsp (20 mL) extra-virgin olive oil

1 clove garlic, chopped

Salt and pepper, to taste

2 (4-inch/10 cm) rounds Brie

3/4 cup (175 mL) oil-packed sun-dried tomatoes, drained and finely chopped

METHOD

Preheat oven to 350°F (180°C). Line a baking sheet with parchment paper.

Bring a large saucepan of salted water to a boil. Place arugula in a fine-mesh sieve and immerse in the boiling water for 30 seconds. Rinse under cold water. Drain and squeeze dry.

In a food processor, combine arugula, pine nuts, olive oil and garlic. Pulse until a thick paste forms. Season with salt and pepper.

Cut away and discard the top rind on each wheel of Brie, keeping the sides intact. Spread top of one with half of arugula mixture and half of sun-dried tomatoes. Repeat with second Brie. Arrange Brie wheels on the baking sheet, at least 2 inches (5 cm) apart.

Bake until cheese is soft in centre, 10 to 12 minutes. Carefully transfer to platters and serve with an assortment of breads.

You can also use Camembert wheels in place of Brie, or get truly decadent and try some pricier cheeses like Brie Supreme or Brie de Meaux.

Use this savoury topping to make another treat—simply cut vertical slices into a baguette, not going all the way through. Stuff some of the arugula mixture into each crevice and bake until bread is warm and crusty.

For a sweeter version, replace this savoury topping with a sweet and nutty one—perfect before or after a meal! Mix together 2 tbsp (25 mL) melted butter, 1/4 cup (50 mL) brown sugar and 1 tsp (5 mL) cinnamon. Press onto top of rounds and sprinkle with 1/2 cup (125 mL) chopped walnuts. Bake as above.

platters, bars & stations

These are a great entertaining solution—easy to put together and guests just serve themselves. They're perfect for informal gatherings, whether it's cocktails, brunch or a do-it-yourself grazing supper.

crudités

Visit your favourite market and check out the range of local, seasonal produce for inspiration. Move beyond carrots and celery—try radicchio, grape tomatoes, new potatoes, asparagus, radishes, baby and heirloom varieties of vegetables . . . the list is endless.

RAW CRUDITÉS

Carrots (organic red and yellow carrots)
Celery
Peppers (red, yellow, green and orange bell peppers, Cubanelles)
Radishes (regular and heirloom varieties, plus daikon radish)
Cucumber (English, regular and baby)
Fennel
Tomatoes (cherry and grape tomatoes in different colours, heirloom varieties)
Mushrooms (button and cremini)
Lettuces (Belgian endive, radicchio, treviso radicchio, baby romaine hearts)
Jicama
Zucchini (green and yellow)

BLANCHED CRUDITÉS

Asparagus (green, white and purple)
String beans (green, yellow and French)
Cauliflower (regular and baby)
Broccoli and broccolini
Rapini
Snow peas and sugar snap peas
Fiddleheads
Potatoes (baby red and white new potatoes, fingerlings)

A SIMPLE PRESENTATION
Stand them up. Veggies look cool standing up. Try those small square glass vases you can buy at a flower store, or other small, clear flower containers (page 52).

BLANCHING VEGETABLES
Some vegetables are much better when they get a quick blanching. (Who really likes their broccoli raw anyway?) Heat up a large pot of salted water until it comes to a rolling boil. Keep a bowl of ice water ready along with a colander in the sink. Place the vegetables in the boiling water until barely tender. Different vegetables take different amounts of time—asparagus takes just a minute or two, whereas new potatoes can take up to 15 minutes—so keep checking to see if your vegetable is just tender but still has the right amount of crunch. As soon as it's ready, drain, then plunge into the ice water to fully cool. Drain again and let dry. And you've got perfectly cooked vegetables with amazing colour.

antipasto platter

There's really nothing to do here but shop for ingredients. Even the most basic of supermarkets has all you need for an antipasto spread. Serve everything on a big platter with some crusty breads and you've got the perfect pre-dinner nibbles, or picnic lunch.

Ask your cheesemonger or deli for help with selections and quantity—they're the experts! Serve the antipasto platter with a variety of fresh breads and drizzle some good olive oil and balsamic vinegar on a plate for dipping.

MEATS
Prosciutto
Pancetta
Salamis (mild and spicy)
Hams (Black Forest, Westphalian, Serrano)
Bresaola, Soppressata

CHEESES
Shaved or crumbled Parmesan
Pecorino, provolone
Soft mozzarella cheese *(bocconcini)*
Feta cheese
Chèvre

VEGETABLES
Marinated olives (green, kalamata, niçoise)
Sun-dried tomatoes
Grilled vegetables (eggplant, zucchini, red onions, bell peppers, portobello mushrooms)
Marinated artichoke hearts
Marinated button or cremini mushrooms
Roasted garlic (page 59)
Slow-roasted Tomatoes (page 189)

panini bar

A casual and versatile entertaining solution is the gourmet panini bar. Set out a sandwich press, some cutting boards, a knife and some cocktail napkins and your friends can assemble their own personalized gourmet panini. Here are some suggested ingredients to get you started.

CHEESES
Shaved Parmesan, mascarpone, soft ricotta, chèvre, Brie, Stilton, Cheddar, feta, Gorgonzola, soft mozzarella *(bocconcini)*, havarti, provolone

FRUITS AND VEGETABLES
Thinly sliced pears and apples, fresh figs, oven-roasted or sun-dried tomatoes, greens (watercress, arugula, baby spinach), fresh herbs (basil, chervil, Italian parsley), grilled vegetables (eggplant, zucchini, red onions), roasted peppers, olives, capers

SPREADS
Pesto, caramelized onions, Dijon, honey mustard or grainy mustard, chutneys and gourmet spreads, flavoured aïolis, bean dips, Sun-dried Tomato and Feta Dip (page 62), tapenade

MEATS
Prosciutto, pancetta, Serrano ham, roasted turkey breast, Black Forest ham, roast beef

BREADS
Bagels, raisin walnut bread, olive bread

. . . and anything else you can think of!

Place the ingredients between two slices of your favourite bread and press in a panini press for a few minutes until toasted. Slice and enjoy a substantial treat!

OTHER COMBOS
Pear and Brie on baguette, apple and old Cheddar with mango chutney on raisin walnut bread

burrito bar

Inspired by Elena Embrioni, our queen of Latin flavour and duchess of sandwiches and fixings. Let your guests mix and match to create their own spicy gourmet delight. Prepare everything ahead—grate cheeses, cut (and grill or roast) veg and meat and put all your spreads in pretty little white bowls. Use soft flour or corn tortillas and either roll (for burritos) or press flat (for quesadillas). Some suggested ingredients . . .

CHEESES
Grated queso fresco, grated Monterey Jack, grated mozzarella, shredded Cheddar, shredded chèvre, grated manchego

VEGETABLES
Roasted peppers (poblanos, red, yellow and green), charred red onions, finely chopped green onions, black beans, kidney beans, roasted tomatoes, cilantro, baby spinach, grilled corn

SPREADS
Salsa, Smoky Tomato Relish (page 162), caramelized onions, sour cream, guacamole, salsa verde

MEATS
Grilled chicken, thinly sliced seared flank steak, top sirloin or skirt steak, shredded pork, cured chorizo sausage, sautéed shrimp (without tails)

. . . and anything else you can think of!

Put all your fixings out on platters and in bowls and let your guests roll up their chosen ingredients in a soft tortilla.

Press burrito or quesadilla in a panini press for a few minutes to warm through, melt cheese and create nice grill marks. Serve with tortilla chips, sour cream, salsa and guacamole, if desired.

pizza bar

Gourmet pizzas are a fun choice for interactive casual gatherings, with endless options. Here are two quick methods for your pizza base . . .

STORE-BOUGHT PIZZA DOUGH

Put a baking sheet in the oven and preheat oven to 400°F (200°C).

On a lightly floured surface, roll out pizza dough to about 1/4 inch (0.5 cm) thick. Use a cookie cutter to cut out the desired sizes of pizzas. Stretch out each dough round even more so it is nice and thin (it will shrink and puff up when baked).

Par-bake the dough rounds. Remove the baking sheet from the oven and sprinkle it with some cornmeal. Lay the dough rounds on the baking sheet and prick the dough all over with a fork. Bake dough rounds for 5 to 7 minutes, just enough for them to firm up. Remove dough rounds from oven and let cool on a rack. (Rounds can be par-baked a few hours ahead.)

When everyone's ready for pizza, preheat oven to 425°F (220°C). Top the par-baked dough rounds with your favourite toppings. Bake just long enough to heat through and to melt the cheese, 5 to 7 minutes.

FLATBREAD PIZZAS

Use store-bought flatbread or your favourite thin pizza shell for the quickest base of all. Add your favourite toppings and bake at 425°F (220°C) until the toppings are heated through and the cheese has melted, 8 to 10 minutes.

Some of my favourite toppings

Caramelized onions, Gorgonzola and fresh thyme

Slow-roasted grape tomatoes, pesto and feta

Chèvre and cream cheese, summer tomatoes and fresh basil

Figs, prosciutto and mascarpone cheese

Pine nuts, Parmesan and baby arugula

Stilton, pear and watercress

Baby spinach, thinly sliced lemon and pancetta

Grilled chicken, fresh rosemary and sun-dried tomatoes

Sautéed mushrooms and Brie

Asparagus, feta and roasted peppers

Top with some good sea salt and a drizzle of good olive oil.

soups

Soups fall into two camps: quick and simple water, veg, cook and hit the table, or classically made with time and love.

If you don't have time for the latter, then you're like most of us, but don't let that stop you from whipping up a quick soup. Simply borrow some of the classic soup techniques: to maximize flavour, sauté your vegetables one at a time; incorporate herbs; use spices like curry and mellow heat like chipotles to give flavour a boost; use homemade stocks when you can; and experiment with finishes like buttermilk or evaporated milk. Use the recipes in this chapter as your template and guide, use up what you have and taste as you go, and you can't go wrong.

Soup truly is the most comforting of all foods, the best way to get veggies into the picky eater, a great way to affordably feed a crowd, the ideal make-ahead dish (always double it and freeze a batch) and a fun way to entertain (think past formal sit-down to stand-up soup station with espresso cups, or even an outdoor winter gathering in take-out coffee cups). Soups are the best way to share your love for food and to say, "Here, I made this for you."

soup basics

stocks

In my grandmother's kitchen, beef stock is lovingly made with roasted beef shanks, and chicken stock from a whole chicken carefully simmered. Vegetable stock involves nothing more than covering vegetables with cold water, tossing in fresh herbs in a bouquet garni and letting it simmer (skimming occasionally) while you go about your day. Butchers, specialty food stores and some supermarkets now carry good-quality stock you can keep in the freezer. If you buy it in the can or box, look for low-sodium brands and stay away from unnecessary additives.

the fat

Butter is the most flavourful fat. In the name of moderation, oils are a more conscientious choice. To cook at higher heats and with healthier fat content, mix butter with a light and flavourful grapeseed, safflower or sunflower seed oil.

soup tools

A chef's knife, a good-sized heavy stockpot, a wooden spoon, and you're ready to create. For purées, hand blenders (immersion blenders) are tidier and quicker than blenders or food processors.

butternut squash and apple soup with maple syrup

This is the perfect soup to serve in fall and winter. Make sure to use good-quality apple cider and real maple syrup—it makes all the difference. My dad makes his own maple syrup every spring. It's my favourite way to naturally sweeten soup. MAKES ABOUT 10 CUPS (2.5 L)

Pepitas are pumpkin seeds. They usually are toasted and often salted and make a delicious snack.

INGREDIENTS

2 medium butternut squash

Kosher salt and pepper, to taste

3 to 4 tbsp (50 to 60 mL) grapeseed or canola oil or butter

2 large cooking onions, diced

1 cup (250 mL) white wine

4 apples (any kind), peeled and roughly chopped

6 cups (1.5 L) unsweetened apple cider

1/2 cup (125 mL) pure maple syrup, plus more for garnish

Tabasco sauce, to taste

Toasted pepitas, for garnish *(see tip)*

METHOD

Preheat oven to 400°F (200°C). Line a baking sheet with parchment paper. Cut squash in half lengthwise and remove seeds. Season squash with salt and pepper. Lay squash cut side down on the baking sheet. Bake until fork tender, 30 to 40 minutes. Let cool slightly.

Heat oil over medium heat in a large, heavy soup pot. Sauté onions for 7 to 10 minutes, stirring often, until translucent. Stir in wine and let the liquid evaporate. Add apple to the pot. Scoop the squash flesh out of the skins and give it a rough chop. Add squash to the pot. Add the cider. Add water if necessary to just barely cover the vegetables. Turn the heat up to medium-high. When the liquid begins to boil, reduce heat and simmer, stirring occasionally, for about 15 minutes, until all vegetables are soft. Remove from heat.

Using a hand (immersion) blender or in a blender, purée soup until it is smooth and silky. Add more water if soup is too thick. Stir in maple syrup and season generously with salt and Tabasco. Pour soup into serving cups and garnish with a drizzle of maple syrup and toasted pepitas.

sweet carrot soup

I make this soup more often than any other. It's very quick to make and packed with flavour. It's sweet, so even the kids might eat it!

MAKES ABOUT 10 CUPS (2.5 L)

This is a quick and simple soup with a vibrant colour. Use it as a base to be creative—ramp up the heat or eliminate curry altogether. You can also take this soup in a Thai direction by using green curry paste in place of curry powder and using coconut milk instead of evaporated milk.

Evaporated milk is a great, inexpensive pantry soup essential for adding depth and sweetness to soups.

INGREDIENTS

3 tbsp (50 mL) grapeseed oil

2 large cooking onions, chopped

1 tbsp (15 mL) mild curry powder

Salt and pepper, to taste

1/2 cup (125 mL) white wine

3 lb (1.5 kg) carrots, peeled and chopped *(about 20 medium carrots)*

6 to 8 cups (1.5 to 2 L) chicken broth *(homemade or store-bought)*

1 can (385 mL) evaporated milk

1 tbsp (15 mL) chopped fresh Italian parsley

METHOD

In a large, heavy soup pot over medium heat, heat oil. Add onions and cook, stirring frequently, until soft, 7 to 10 minutes. Stir in curry powder. Cook, stirring frequently, for a few minutes until fragrant, then season with salt and pepper. Stir in wine, scraping up any bits that have stuck to the bottom of the pan, and let it evaporate (turn up heat if necessary).

Add carrots and cook for 3 to 5 minutes. Add enough broth to just cover the carrots and simmer until they are soft (about 20 minutes). Remove from heat.

Using a hand (immersion) blender or in a blender, purée soup until it is very smooth. Season to taste. Stir in evaporated milk. Garnish with parsley. Serve hot.

cool roasted red pepper and buttermilk soup

This soup is packed with flavour, and the buttermilk gives the impression of richness—but you can have seconds guilt-free.

MAKES ABOUT 10 CUPS (2.5 L)

INGREDIENTS

8 large red bell peppers
1/4 cup (50 mL) butter
2 cups (500 mL) thinly sliced leeks *(about 3 leeks)*
1/2 cup (125 mL) chopped celery
1/4 cup (50 mL) chopped carrots
4 to 6 cups (1 to 1.5 L) chicken stock
Sprig each of fresh thyme and parsley
1 cup (250 mL) buttermilk
Honey (optional)
Salt and pepper, to taste

METHOD

Roast red peppers directly over a gas flame, turning often, until charred on all sides (or place peppers on a baking sheet and roast them under the broiler, turning often, until the skins are blackened and charred). Place peppers in plastic bags and seal bags. When peppers are cool enough to handle, peel off the skins and discard. Remove seeds and stems and discard. Chop peppers roughly and set aside.

Melt butter in a large, heavy soup pot over medium-high heat. Add leeks and cook until golden (about 10 minutes). Add celery and carrots. Cook, stirring occasionally, for another 10 minutes. Add red peppers. Add chicken stock, scraping up any bits that have stuck to the bottom of the pan. Add herb sprigs. Bring to a boil, reduce heat and simmer for 20 minutes or until all vegetables are soft. Remove from heat.

Discard herb sprigs. Using a hand (immersion) blender or in a blender, purée soup until smooth. Stir in buttermilk and season with salt and pepper. If soup is too acidic, add a few tablespoons of honey to balance the flavour. This soup is also delicious hot.

Yes, you can use store-bought roasted red peppers to save time. They're not as smoky and flavourful, but only you can place a value on your time! Make sure to rinse them very well in a colander—they usually come packed in a vinegar bath that needs to be rinsed off well.

My mother-in-law makes a delicious variation by simply sautéing raw red peppers, using stock and finishing with cream. She keeps it in a pitcher as a ready-to-go summer lunch.

sweet potato chipotle soup

A perfect balance of sweet and heat with a smoky undertone—good for you too! MAKES ABOUT 10 CUPS (2.5 L)

Chipotle peppers are smoked jalapeños with a deep smoky flavour. Chipotles can be found dried or canned in adobo sauce. Most supermarkets carry the canned chipotles in the Mexican food section.

Maple syrup and honey are interchangeable sweeteners for soups.

INGREDIENTS

2 to 3 large sweet potatoes *(about 2 lb/1 kg)*
3 tbsp (50 mL) grapeseed or canola oil or butter
2 large cooking onions, diced
1 cup (250 mL) white wine
1 chipotle pepper in adobo sauce, finely minced, adobo sauce reserved
6 to 8 cups (1.5 to 2 L) cold water or vegetable or chicken stock
1/4 cup (50 mL) honey or maple syrup, or more to taste
Salt, to taste

METHOD

Preheat oven to 375°F (190°C). Line a baking sheet with foil. Place whole sweet potatoes on the baking sheet. Bake sweet potatoes until they are soft when pierced with a fork (about 1 hour). Let cool. Peel off and discard the skin and give the potato flesh a rough chop.

Heat oil over medium heat in a large, heavy soup pot. Cook onions for 7 to 10 minutes, stirring often, until translucent. Stir in wine. When liquid has evaporated, add chipotle and sweet potatoes to the pot. Add cold water to just barely cover the veg.

Turn the heat up to medium-high. When the water begins to boil, reduce heat and simmer for 20 minutes or until vegetables are soft.

Remove from heat. Using a hand (immersion) blender or in a blender, carefully purée soup until it is smooth and silky. Stir in honey and season generously with salt and reserved adobo sauce.

elena's caldo verde

Our executive chef Elena Embrioni makes seriously flavourful soups.
It may have something to do with over 20 years' experience in the kitchen
and strong Latin American roots bringing wonderful ingredients and
flavours to the forefront. This Portuguese chorizo and kale soup is a
prime example. MAKES ABOUT 6 CUPS (1.5 L)

INGREDIENTS

2 tbsp (25 mL) olive oil

2 medium onions, chopped

3 medium Yukon Gold potatoes, peeled and diced

6 cloves garlic, minced

2 bay leaves

1 lb (500 g) kale, coarsely chopped

Salt and pepper, to taste

1 can (14 oz/398 mL) navy beans

1 can (14 oz/398 mL) diced tomatoes

1 lb (500 g) dry chorizo, sliced crosswise into ¼ inch pieces

4 cups (1 L) chicken broth

¼ cup (50 mL) chopped parsley

METHOD

Heat oil in deep pot over medium heat. Add onions and cook for 5 minutes
until caramelized. Add potatoes and garlic, cover and cook 5 minutes,
stirring occasionally.

Add bay leaves and kale to the pot and cover for 2 minutes to wilt greens. Add salt
and pepper and stir in beans, tomatoes, chorizo and broth. Bring soup to a boil
and reduce heat to a simmer until potatoes are tender. Stir in parsley and serve
with warm crusty bread such as a Portuguese corn bread or sourdough boule.

SPECIAL OCCASIONS

═══════

duo of gazpachos

chilled petits pois purée with lemon crème fraîche

roasted cauliflower soup with stilton

parsnip, celery root and green apple soup

woodland mushroom soup

jump-up soup

duo of gazpachos

These cold soups make a perfect refreshing light summer lunch. Serve in shot glasses as a duo for an elegant starter or hors d'oeuvre, or on their own with some great bread.

green gazpacho

MAKES ABOUT 10 CUPS (2.5 L)

INGREDIENTS

4 cups (1 L) chopped cucumber, not peeled
4 cups (1 L) washed, chopped romaine lettuce
1 cup (250 mL) chopped green pepper
1/2 cup (125 mL) chopped red onion
2 medium poblano peppers, chopped
2 cloves garlic, chopped
½ bunch cilantro, chopped
2 cups (500 mL) cubed day-old white bread
¼ cup (50 mL) sherry vinegar (or to taste)
¼ cup (50 mL) extra virgin olive oil (or to taste)
4 cups (1 L) (approx) vegetable stock or water
Salt and pepper

METHOD

Combine all ingredients except stock in a large bowl and let sit for 1 hour.
Blend in batches with hand blender with enough vegetable stock or water to achieve desired consistency. Chill for a few hours before serving. Adjust seasoning.
To serve, pour in bowls or glasses.

Try serving this with a grilled shrimp hanging off the edge of the glass or bowl.

tomato gazpacho

MAKES ABOUT 10 CUPS (2.5 L)

INGREDIENTS

2 lbs (1 kg) ripe tomatoes, halved
2 cups (500 mL) canned tomatoes
2 cups (500 mL) large chunks of day-old white country bread
1 medium red pepper, roughly chopped
1 English cucumber, peeled, chopped
1 cup (250 mL) chopped red onion
1 zucchini, chopped
1 clove garlic, chopped
½ tsp (2 mL) cumin
½ tsp (2 mL) paprika
¼ cup (50 mL) sherry vinegar
¼ cup (50 mL) extra virgin olive oil
Salt and pepper
½ cup (125 mL) chopped parsley

METHOD

Roughly chop the fresh and canned tomatoes. Combine tomatoes, bread, pepper, cucumber, onion, zucchini, garlic, cumin and paprika and let sit for 1 hour.
Blend in batches with hand blender with enough water to achieve smooth consistency. Add sherry vinegar, oil, salt and pepper to taste. Chill for a few hours before serving.
To serve, pour in bowls or glasses and garnish with chopped parsley and a drizzle of oil.

chilled petits pois purée with lemon crème fraîche

This soup is one of Sacha's most popular dishes in our entertaining cooking classes. It's a refreshing starter for an elegant dinner, or you can serve it at your next cocktail party in little shot glasses. Pass the sweet pea shooters around to your guests on a long tray lined with a white linen napkin for a cool and different hors d'oeuvre. MAKES 11 CUPS (2.75 L)

Make sure you get this soup silky smooth—have some patience when you purée it. Adjust the amount of liquid to get the right consistency.

This soup is at its best the day it is blended—the colour starts to fade after that. You can blanch the peas and sauté the leeks the day before, and just blend ingredients the day of for a stress-free party soup.

Another great garnish idea— crispy cooked pancetta.

INGREDIENTS

Soup

3 tbsp (50 mL) butter
1 leek *(white and light green part)*, washed, trimmed and chopped
4 shallots, chopped
1 onion, chopped
1 bag (1 kg) frozen petits pois
Leaves from 1 bunch mint, chopped
6 cups (1.5 L) vegetable stock or water
1 tbsp (15 mL) vinegar *(Champagne, white wine or sherry)*
Kosher salt and pepper, to taste

Lemon Crème Fraîche

Zest of 2 lemons
1/2 cup (125 mL) crème fraîche or sour cream

METHOD

Melt butter in a medium sauté pan over medium heat and cook leek, shallots and onion, stirring occasionally, until translucent, 5 to 10 minutes. Set aside to cool.

Bring a large pot of salted water to a rolling boil. Have ready a large bowl of ice water. Add peas to the boiling water and blanch for 30 seconds. Immediately drain peas and quickly transfer them to the ice water. Let cool completely, then drain again.

Combine leek mixture, peas, mint and cold vegetable stock in a large pot or bowl. Using a hand (immersion) blender or in a blender, thoroughly purée soup until it is very smooth. Add vinegar. Season generously with salt and pepper. Chill.

To make the Lemon Crème Fraîche, stir lemon zest into crème fraîche. Place a ladleful of soup in a bowl. Top with a dollop of Lemon Crème Fraîche.

roasted cauliflower soup
with stilton

This is an impressive soup for the host looking to make a statement—
without breaking the bank. MAKES ABOUT 8 CUPS (2 L)

INGREDIENTS

5 cups (1.25 L) 1-inch (2.5 cm) cauliflower florets
   (from 1 medium cauliflower)
3 tbsp (50 mL) olive oil
Salt and pepper, to taste
1/4 cup (50 mL) unsalted butter
2 large onions, chopped
2 leeks (white part only), chopped
1/2 cup (125 mL) white wine
4 to 6 cups (1 to 1.5 L) vegetable or chicken stock or water
A splash of vinegar *(sherry, white wine or Champagne)*
1/2 cup (125 mL) crumbled Stilton (3 oz/90 g), for garnish

Roasting vegetables for a soup
really enhances the flavour— try
this technique with carrots, butternut squash or parsnips. Roasted
cauliflower is also a delicious side
dish in its own right!

METHOD

Preheat oven to 400°F (200°C). Put cauliflower florets onto a large baking sheet
   and lightly coat with olive oil, salt and pepper. Roast until light golden (about
   25 minutes).
Melt butter in a large, heavy soup pot over medium heat. Cook onions and leeks, stirring occasionally, until softened but not browned, 5 to 7 minutes. Season with a bit
   of salt. Add white wine and cook, stirring, until liquid is evaporated.
Add roasted cauliflower. Add enough stock to barely cover the vegetables. Turn up
   the heat to medium-high and simmer soup for about 15 minutes or until vegetables are soft.
Remove from heat. Using a hand (immersion) blender or in a blender, purée soup
   until it is very smooth. If the soup is too thick, add a bit more liquid until you reach
   the desired consistency. Season with salt, pepper and a splash of vinegar, to taste.
Serve soup in bowls and top with a pile of crumbled Stilton.

parsnip, celery root and green apple soup

This is a deep, intense soup that is perfect if you are looking for a special first course to impress guests. MAKES ABOUT 10 CUPS (2.5 L)

Feel free to use pears in this recipe instead of apples.

For an elegant presentation, drizzle with herb and pumpkin-seed oils and top with a very fine julienne (or small dice) of Granny Smith apple and toasted pepitas.

INGREDIENTS

3 to 4 tbsp (50 to 60 mL) grapeseed or canola oil or butter
2 large cooking onions, chopped
1 cup (250 mL) white wine
1 large celery root, peeled and roughly chopped
5 Granny Smith apples, peeled and roughly chopped
2 large parsnips, peeled and roughly chopped
6 to 8 cups (1.5 to 2 L) cold water or vegetable stock
Kosher salt and freshly ground pepper, to taste
1 to 2 tbsp (15 to 25 mL) vinegar *(apple cider, Champagne or white wine)*
1 cup (250 mL) 35% cream *(optional)*

METHOD

Heat oil over medium heat in a large, heavy soup pot. Cook onions for 5 to 10 minutes, until translucent. Stir in wine and let the liquid evaporate. Add celery root, apples and parsnips. Add cold water to just barely cover the vegetables. Turn the heat up to medium-high. When the water begins to boil, reduce heat and simmer until vegetables are tender, 15 to 20 minutes. Remove from heat.

Using a hand (immersion) blender or in a blender, purée soup until it is smooth and silky. Season generously with salt and pepper. Add a dash of vinegar to help "awaken" the flavour even more. Add cream, if desired. Serve hot.

salads

This chapter showcases a number of different salads, but when it comes to casual entertaining, the salad I most often serve at home really doesn't have a recipe, and it has only a few ingredients.

What matters is the quality of these ingredients. Now's the time to bring out your best-quality extra-virgin olive oil and good flaky sea salt—they make all the difference! After years of hunting, we discovered and now sell our own dish eight-year-old balsamic vinegar from Modena and first-pressed Greek olive oil—kitchen must-haves and the perfect host gift!

Simply buy the freshest seasonal greens you can find—mix and match varieties or highlight just one. Wash and spin dry. When ready to serve, place greens in a bowl, give them a good pinch of sea salt and a few turns of the peppermill, a good squirt of fresh lemon juice and a few glugs of top-quality olive oil. Toss and taste it to make sure you have the right balance. And there you have the perfect simple green salad. For a change, add some shavings of Parmigiano-Reggiano or replace the lemon juice with aged balsamic vinegar. And remember—the fewer ingredients you use, the better quality they should be, so don't scrimp on the oil, salt and vinegar.

Have fun mixing in fresh fruits (like the apples with smoked trout and pears in the pear carpaccio salad) or nuts (pine nuts pair beautifully with the grilled asparagus and pistachios are pretty and different in the arugula salad). Make it a meal with cheeses (from mild mozzarella to intense Stilton). And of course mix up your greens to keep things interesting.

salad basics

the balance

I like to use 1 part acid or vinegar to 2 to 3 parts oil. For nice and tart, try a 1-to-2 ratio, and for more oily, 1-to-3. Always start with your base and emulsifier (mustard, shallots, etc.), then slowly whisk in the oil to bind your vinaigrette into an emulsion. Your vinaigrette won't separate and will last for days, refrigerated.

bases

Vinegars or acids: For intense, bigger flavours with greens like arugula, frisée or radicchio, use balsamic or tarragon vinegar. For mid-intensity salads, try red wine, white wine, sherry or Champagne vinegar. For a lighter, fresh base, try fresh lemon or lime juice (add the zest for extra flavour).

emulsifiers and flavours

To bind your dressings together and give a thicker consistency, add Dijon or your favourite mustard to a more intense vinaigrette, sugar to a lighter vinaigrette, or sour cream or mayo to a creamy dressing. Fresh herbs like tarragon are wonderful additions.

oils

Olive oil is the grandfather of all oils. Look to different origins (Greece, Italy) and opt for first-pressed (the purest). I like olive oil best in dressings. Light, fruity alternatives include grapeseed, safflower, sunflower, canola or vegetable oil (which are also great pantry essentials for high-heat cooking).

the role of salt

Wonder why restaurant salads taste so good? Salt! Salting your lettuce pulls out the flavour. Use kosher salt and/or finish with a flaked salt like Maldon sea salt to give a crunch.

When dressing your salad, put dressing in bottom of bowl and be sure to hold back some lettuce. Dress just before serving, then if you overdress, add more lettuce.

LETTUCE STORAGE—As soon as you get home from the store, wash and spin dry well. Loosely wrap in paper towels or a clean tea towel and keep in the crisper.

TYPES OF DRESSINGS—If you get bored with the same old dressing night after night, try rotating between a simple oil-and-vinegar, an emulsified vinaigrette, a creamy dressing, a cooked dressing or a blender emulsion. Sweeten up the dressing with maple syrup or sugar (best with fruits).

MIXING IT UP—All it takes to receive rave reviews is to have fun with what you toss into your salad—dried fruits (cranberries, apricots, apples, pears), fresh fruits presented nicely (thinly sliced pears, finely diced apples), toasted nuts and seeds (sunflower, almonds, cashews) and of course cheeses, all sorts of cheeses. Reach past the romaine and try a variety of lettuces best found at a specialty greengrocer.

EVERYDAY SIMPLE

balsamic potato salad

lemon orzo salad with baby spinach,
feta and caramelized onion

tomato and bread salad

grilled corn salad

greek isle salad with pickled red onion

watermelon, feta and pine nut salad

caesar salad with crisp pancetta and
roasted garlic vinaigrette

baby spinach salad with lemon,
strawberries and pine nuts

balsamic potato salad

This is an old recipe from one of my very first catering clients. She gave me her own recipe to prepare for her guests, and it worked beautifully. It's simple and straightforward, and I love this non-mayo version. Perfect for a picnic or casual buffet. SERVES 8

INGREDIENTS

2 lb (1 kg) unpeeled baby red potatoes, halved
1/4 cup (50 mL) olive oil
1 red onion, thinly sliced
1/4 cup (50 mL) balsamic vinegar
1 tbsp (15 mL) mustard seeds
1 tbsp (15 mL) Dijon mustard
Salt and pepper, to taste
2 tbsp (25 mL) finely minced chives *(or 4 green onions, sliced diagonally)*

METHOD

Cover potatoes with salted water and boil until tender but not soft. Drain. Set aside 1 1/2 tsp (7 mL) olive oil. Put warm potatoes in a large bowl and gently toss with remaining olive oil.

Heat the 1 1/2 tsp (7 mL) oil in a sauté pan over medium heat. Cook onion, stirring often, until tender but still pink (about 15 minutes). Remove onion from pan and set aside.

Return pan to heat and deglaze with balsamic vinegar and a little water. Add mustard seeds and Dijon. Stir until mixture forms a paste.

Toss potatoes with balsamic mixture and reserved onion. Season with salt and pepper and decorate with chives.

lemon orzo salad
with baby spinach, feta
and caramelized onion

In my early catering days with my friend Foofie, most of the parties were for casual crowds on islands, in fields, in precarious places! We needed dishes that could stand up to bumpy travel and the test of time. Most of my casual salads are make-ahead, are great for a crowd and don't require last-minute fuss (you have enough to do!). This is a Georgian Bay island favourite. SERVES 10 TO 12

INGREDIENTS

2 cups (500 mL) orzo

3 tbsp (50 mL) vegetable oil

2 red onions, thinly sliced

2 cloves garlic, minced

Salt and pepper, to taste

12 oz (375 g) feta cheese, cut into 1/2-inch (1 cm) cubes

8 cups (2 L) loosely packed baby spinach, washed

1/2 cup (125 mL) olive oil

Zest and juice of 2 lemons

This salad can be made 2 days in advance and stored, covered and refrigerated. Bring to room temperature before serving.

METHOD

Cook orzo in a pot of boiling salted water until al dente. Drain and rinse under cold water to stop cooking. Toss with 1 tbsp (15 mL) of the vegetable oil. Set aside.

Heat a large sauté pan over medium-high heat. Add remaining 2 tbsp (25 mL) vegetable oil and sliced onions. Cook onions, stirring often, for 10 minutes. Add up to 1 tbsp more oil if pan becomes dry. Reduce heat to medium-low, add garlic and continue to cook, stirring often, for another 15 to 20 minutes, until onions are golden. Remove from heat and season with salt and pepper. Let cool.

In a large bowl, combine orzo with feta, spinach, olive oil, lemon zest and juice and caramelized onions. Season with salt and pepper and toss to mix.

tomato and bread salad

This is one of those salads that is hard to commit to paper, since there are so many wonderful versions. Leila created a Middle Eastern fattoush using toasted pita and exotic spices like sumac and zaatar. The casual Italian version, panzanella, calls for torn bread. Elena and Sacha mastered this perfect simple panzanella that truly represents seaside Italy and good living. SERVES 12

This rustic salad is very simple to make but its goodness depends on the quality of two ingredients—the tomatoes and the vinegar. Use a top-quality vinegar and make this only with ripe, flavourful tomatoes.

INGREDIENTS

1 baguette or boule, cut into 1-inch (2.5 cm) cubes
3 tbsp (50 mL) olive oil
2 large ripe tomatoes, cut into wedges
1 English cucumber, cut into 1-inch (2.5 cm) cubes
1 yellow bell pepper, cut into 1-inch (2.5 cm) cubes
1/2 red onion, cut in half lengthwise and thinly sliced
20 large basil leaves, coarsely chopped

Vinaigrette
1 clove garlic, minced
1 tsp (5 mL) Dijon mustard
1/4 cup (50 mL) sherry vinegar *(or red wine vinegar)*
1/2 cup (125 mL) olive oil
Salt and pepper, to taste

METHOD

Preheat oven to 350°F (180°C). Toss bread cubes in olive oil. Place on a baking sheet. Toast bread, stirring occasionally, until golden brown (about 10 minutes). Let cool. Whisk vinaigrette ingredients together in a bowl until emulsified. Season to taste.

In a large bowl, combine bread cubes, tomatoes, cucumber, yellow pepper, red onion and basil. Add vinaigrette and toss well. Season with lots of salt and pepper. Let sit for at least 30 minutes before serving so the bread can soak up all the juices.

grilled corn salad

When I was growing up, we spent some summers at my dad's family cottage, and my grandmother Dodie always had corn on the cob on hand. Inevitably we would have leftovers, and my grandmother introduced me to cold corn. To this day, cold corn still rivals the hot. This salad is a wonderful summer accompaniment to any grilled chicken, meat or fish—almost like a salsa or relish. When you're a little tired of corn on the cob, this makes a terrific alternative. SERVES 6

The corn and poblanos can be prepared the day before, and the salad can be assembled a few hours ahead.

Poblano peppers are relatively mild, dark green chili peppers about half the size of a bell pepper (the larger the pepper, the milder it usually is). They can be found in Latin markets and some grocery stores. If you can't find poblanos, use a jalapeño pepper instead. Jalapeños are smaller and pack more punch, so be careful! For a milder substitute, use a Cubanelle pepper or two (it looks like a long, thin, light green bell pepper).

INGREDIENTS

1 large poblano pepper
4 ears corn, husked
1 pint cherry tomatoes, halved
1 small red onion, finely chopped
1/2 bunch fresh cilantro, finely chopped
1 clove garlic, finely minced
1/4 cup (50 mL) extra-virgin olive oil
1/4 cup (50 mL) fresh lime juice
Salt and pepper, to taste

METHOD

Preheat grill to high. Roast poblano on the hot grill, turning often, until skin is blistered and black. (You can also do this over a gas burner or under a broiler.) Do not turn off the grill.

Place poblano in a small bowl and cover with plastic wrap. When poblano is cool enough to handle, slip off skin and remove seeds. Slice roasted poblano into long, thin strips.

In a large pot of boiling salted water, blanch corn for 1 minute. Place corn on the hot grill. Grill, turning corn often to develop a bit of char on the surface but not enough to burn it (about 5 minutes). Let cool. Carefully slice kernels off each cob and into a large bowl.

Add poblano, cherry tomatoes, red onion, cilantro and garlic. Toss with olive oil, lime juice, salt and pepper.

greek isle salad
with pickled red onion

Sacha created this salad for her "Greek Island" class. Lisa, another dish teacher, introduced me to this simplest-ever technique for pickling onions, which keeps flavours light and colours brilliant. SERVES 6

INGREDIENTS

Pickled Onion

1 small red onion, halved lengthwise and thinly sliced
1/2 cup (125 mL) fresh lime juice

Vinaigrette

1/2 cup (125 mL) extra-virgin olive oil
1/4 cup (50 mL) red wine vinegar
3 tbsp (50 mL) chopped fresh oregano
Salt and freshly ground black pepper, to taste

Salad

8 oz (250 g) feta cheese, cut into 3/4-inch (2 cm) cubes
2 cups (500 mL) cherry or grape tomatoes, halved
1 yellow or orange bell pepper, cut into 1-inch (2.5 cm) pieces
1 English cucumber, cut into half-moons
1/4 cup (50 mL) finely chopped Italian parsley
Salt and pepper, to taste

This is a slightly more elegant version of the classic Greek village salad. The pickled red onion is a breeze to make and adds incredible flavour and a gorgeous deep pink colour to the salad. You can make it several days ahead of time and store it in the fridge in the lime juice (you can also use lemon juice). Double or triple the recipe and have it handy to put in sandwiches, burritos and salsas or on burgers, or as a simple accompaniment to meat.

Leftover vinaigrette keeps, covered and refrigerated, up to 1 week.

METHOD

To make the pickled onion, place onion in a large bowl. Add lime juice and stir together. Let marinate for 30 minutes, stirring often.

To make the vinaigrette, whisk together olive oil, vinegar and oregano in a bowl to blend. Season.

Drain onion and return to bowl. Add feta, tomatoes, bell pepper, cucumber and parsley. Toss with enough vinaigrette to coat. Season with salt and pepper to taste.

watermelon, feta and pine nut salad

In the summer months, watermelon is always in the house, but some-times it's hard to plow through the whole thing. As a result, I've turned it into a simple salad—a refreshing and innovative way to feed a crowd. (Even kids love it—minus the pine nuts.) SERVES 6

If you can find ricotta salata, a hard, salty variety of ricotta cheese, try some of that instead of the feta.

To make a chiffonade, stack up herb leaves, roll tightly and cut on an angle to produce thin ribbons without bruising the herb.

INGREDIENTS

5 cups (1.25 L) seeded watermelon cubes (about 1 inch/2.5 cm)
1/2 cup (125 mL) pine nuts, lightly toasted
8 oz (250 g) feta cheese, cut into 1-inch (2.5 cm) cubes
1/4 cup (50 mL) fresh mint leaves, cut in chiffonade *(see tip)*
2 tbsp (25 mL) extra-virgin olive oil
1 tbsp (15 mL) fresh lemon juice
Salt, to taste

METHOD

In a large bowl, combine watermelon, pine nuts, feta and mint. Toss with oil and lemon juice to lightly coat. Season with salt. Serve immediately.

SPECIAL OCCASIONS

baby greens with smoked trout
and green apple

asian slaw

asparagus salad with pine nuts,
parmesan and grilled lemon vinaigrette

caprese salad with summer tomatoes
and soft mozzarella with pesto

salade chèvre chaude with croûtes

sunshine salad with passion fruit and
poppy seed vinaigrette

boston lettuce and pear carpaccio salad

baby arugula with baby beets,
feta and pistachios

asian slaw

This recipe was adapted from the intricate slaw chef Greg Couillard made at our original Chinatown-tour cooking classes, when dish first opened in Toronto. Greg introduced me to interesting exotic fruits and vegetables and innovative ways to prepare them. This recipe is a simple variation—vibrant, crunchy and delicious. SERVES 8 TO 10

I like to serve this salad in cute white Chinese food take-out containers with funky chopsticks (see the cover photo)—these party items can be found easily in Asian markets. While you are there, stock up on Asian pantry essentials like sweet chili sauce, fish sauce, sriracha, sambal chili paste and other great condiments! A lot of these items can now be found in larger grocery stores, but I prefer visiting Chinatown for a fun, inspiring shopping experience.

INGREDIENTS

Slaw

2 ripe but firm mangoes, peeled and julienned

1 small head red cabbage, shredded or thinly sliced

1 head baby bok choy, core removed, cut in chiffonade

1 red bell pepper, thinly sliced

4 carrots, peeled and grated or julienned

2 cups (500 mL) bean sprouts

3 green onions, finely sliced diagonally

Leaves from 1/2 bunch cilantro, roughly chopped

1/2 cup (125 mL) dry-roasted peanuts, roughly chopped

Vinaigrette

Juice of 4 limes

2 tbsp (25 mL) Asian sweet chili sauce

2 tbsp (25 mL) fish sauce

4 tsp (20 mL) sugar

1/4 cup (50 mL) vegetable oil

METHOD

Combine mangoes, cabbage, baby bok choy, red pepper, carrots, bean sprouts and green onions in a large bowl. In a separate bowl, whisk together lime juice, chili sauce, fish sauce and sugar. Slowly drizzle in oil, whisking constantly. Pour vinaigrette over the vegetables and mix thoroughly. Refrigerate and let marinate for up to 1 hour. Serve garnished with cilantro and chopped peanuts.

asparagus salad with pine nuts, parmesan and lemon vinaigrette

This salad is a spring favourite. Featuring seasonal ingredients at their best, it's simple and beautiful. SERVES 6

INGREDIENTS

Grilled Lemon Vinaigrette
2 lemons, halved crosswise
1 tbsp (15 mL) Dijon mustard
1 shallot, finely diced
1/2 cup (125 mL) extra-virgin olive oil
1 to 2 tbsp (15 to 25 mL) honey
Salt and freshly ground pepper, to taste

Salad
2 lb (1 kg) asparagus, trimmed
  of woody ends
1/4 cup (50 mL) extra-virgin olive oil
1/2 cup (125 mL) pine nuts, toasted
7-oz (200 g) piece Parmigiano-
  Reggiano cheese, shaved

METHOD

Heat a grill pan or broiler to high. Juice lemons over a small bowl, using a sieve to catch the seeds. Add Dijon and shallot and whisk to combine. Slowly whisk in 1/2 cup (125 mL) oil, a little at a time, until emulsified. Whisk in honey and season with salt and pepper.

Toss asparagus with 1/4 cup (50 mL) oil and salt and pepper to taste. Place on hot grill. Grill for 4 to 6 minutes, turning once, until tender and just cooked through. (Grilled asparagus can be served at room temperature or hot.) Divide asparagus among 6 plates, in a nice centred pile with all the tips facing in the same direction. Drizzle some of the lemon vinaigrette on the asparagus and around the plate. Sprinkle with pine nuts and some Parmesan shavings. Top with a final seasoning of good sea salt and freshly ground pepper. (Or serve this salad family-style on a big platter for a less formal presentation.)

Grilled lemon vinaigrette can be made up to 2 days in advance; whisk again to emulsify before using. Asparagus can be grilled earlier in the day and served at room temperature.

Use pecorino, feta or chèvre in place of the shaved Parmesan cheese.

Alternatively, oven roast the asparagus with a bit of oil at 500°F (260°C) for approximately 5 minutes till just cooked through.

A simpler version of this salad turns it into an easy side dish—just grill your asparagus and drizzle with good olive oil and a squeeze of lemon. Serve alongside grilled chicken, fish or steak.

This flavour combo is one of my quick mid-week dinner favourites—stir cooked angel hair pasta with some reserved pasta water and cheese to melt (I love it with feta, chèvre or Parmesan), the grilled asparagus, toasted nuts and a bit of oil and lemon juice. When the pasta is still piping hot, you can also toss in some baby arugula.

salade chèvre chaude with croûtes

Years ago, I was fortunate enough to be a guest in a French farmhouse for lunch. We were served this salad. The only warm salad I'd had before then was my mom and grandmother's "Dutch lettuce," made with bacon drippings, cream and white vinegar. Don't analyze the fat content, just pour yourself a glass of wine and enjoy it. This salad is a perfect winter entertaining dish. It says Old World comfort, and is great when the usual salad ingredients are not at their best. SERVES 6

LARDONS: ask your butcher for a slab of double-smoked bacon. Cut it yourself (or ask your butcher to cut it) into 1/2-inch (1 cm) thick slices.

You can use clean fishing line to cut chèvre, if you like.

CROÛTES: preheat oven to 375°F (190°C). Lay 6 baguette slices (cut on the diagonal) on a baking sheet and bake until golden (about 10 minutes). Rub with a halved garlic clove and drizzle with olive oil; sprinkle with salt.

INGREDIENTS

4-oz (125 g) log soft chèvre, chilled
Olive oil, to taste
Cracked black pepper, to taste
6 croûtes *(see tip)*
6 strips thick bacon or lardons, cut into 1/2-inch (1 cm) pieces
3 tbsp (50 mL) good-quality balsamic vinegar
2 tsp (10 mL) Dijon mustard
2 heads frisée lettuce, trimmed, washed and dried
Salt, to taste

METHOD

Preheat oven to 400°F (200°C). Using a sharp knife or unflavoured dental floss, cut chèvre crosswise into 6 slices.

Place chèvre discs on the baking sheet; drizzle with olive oil and sprinkle with cracked pepper. Bake chèvre until it is just soft and a bit golden, 3 to 5 minutes. Using a spatula, transfer chèvre rounds to top of each croûte.

Cook bacon in a skillet over medium heat until crispy. Remove and set aside. Save 3 tbsp (50 mL) of the warm bacon fat in the pan, discarding the rest. Add balsamic vinegar to the warm fat. Remove from heat and whisk in mustard. Keep warm.

Season frisée lettuce with salt and pepper. Toss lettuce with warm vinaigrette to coat (frisée will wilt a bit). Place a mound of salad on each plate and top with bacon.

Place a chèvre-topped croûte on each plate and serve immediately.

sunshine salad with passion fruit and poppy seed vinaigrette

This salad was inspired by a stay at Mon Caprice Villa in Barbados, where tropical fruits played a cool and refreshing role in many dishes. Bring the Islands home with this pretty, fresh salad, brought to life by an unusual passion fruit vinaigrette. SERVES 8

INGREDIENTS

Vinaigrette

2 passion fruits

Zest and juice of 1/2 orange

1 tbsp (15 mL) red wine vinegar

1/2 tsp (2 mL) honey cup or Russian
 sweet mustard

1/2 cup (125 mL) canola or
 grapeseed oil

2 tbsp (25 mL) honey

1 tbsp (15 mL) poppy seeds

Salt, to taste

Salad

1 English cucumber

2 ripe mangoes

2 papayas, peeled, seeds removed

1 small red onion

1 bunch watercress

Passion fruits are small, round fruits native to southern climates. They are usually a purple colour but can sometimes be orange or yellow. Their skins are inedible, but the pulpy inside yields a juicy, slightly tart flavour. Look for passion fruits with unbruised, wrinkly skins—this means they are ripe and ready to eat. You can find passion fruits in Latin markets, and many supermarkets carry them in their exotic-fruit section. If you can't find passion fruits, simply omit them from the vinaigrette.

METHOD

Cut cucumber, mangoes and papayas into matchsticks about 2 inches (5 cm) long. Slice red onion very thinly.

Cut passion fruits in half and scoop out and discard seeds. In a food processor, pulse passion fruit flesh until smooth. Add orange zest and juice, vinegar and mustard. Blend together. With machine running, slowly add oil through feed tube until emulsified. Remove blade (or transfer to a bowl) and stir in honey and poppy seeds. Season with salt.

Carefully toss watercress with some of the vinaigrette and arrange on plates. Lightly coat fruit and vegetable matchsticks with some of the vinaigrette and pile on top. Serve immediately.

baby arugula with baby beets, feta and pistachios

An abundant seasonal salad that works as a meal. SERVES 6

If you can't find hazelnut oil, use 1/2 cup (125 mL) grapeseed oil.

Once the beets are cool enough to handle, using a paring knife, cut off the tops and peel off the skins with your fingers. I suggest wearing rubber gloves, unless you like purple hands!

I love baby beets for their vibrant colour and subtle taste (far less earthy than regular beets). You can find them at specialty grocers and farmers' markets.

INGREDIENTS

3 bunches baby beets *(red, yellow, striped or a combo)*
Salt and freshly ground pepper, to taste
1 shallot, finely diced
1/4 cup (50 mL) sherry or red wine vinegar
1 tsp (5 mL) Dijon mustard
1/4 cup (50 mL) hazelnut oil *(see tip)*
1/4 cup (50 mL) grapeseed oil
1 tbsp (15 mL) honey
6 cups (1.5 L) baby arugula
10 oz (300 g) feta cheese, shaved
1/2 cup (125 mL) pistachios, toasted and roughly chopped *(not the dyed ones, please!)*

METHOD

Preheat oven to 400°F (200°C). Wash beets and trim off any leafy greens. Do not peel. Place beets in a baking dish, add about 1/2 inch (1 cm) of water and season with salt and pepper. Cover with foil and bake for 30 to 45 minutes or until beets are just tender when pierced with a knife. (Baking time will depend on the size of the beets.) Let cool.

Peel the beets (the skins will now slip off easily; see tip). Cut each beet in half lengthwise (or leave whole depending on size) and transfer to a bowl. Set aside.

In a small bowl, whisk together shallot, vinegar and Dijon. Slowly whisk in the oils, a little at a time, until emulsified. Whisk in honey and season with salt and pepper. Drizzle some of the vinaigrette on the beets and season them with salt and pepper; toss gently. In a separate bowl, gently toss baby arugula with some of the vinaigrette and season with salt and pepper.

Evenly divide dressed greens among plates. Place a few beet halves around each pile of greens. Top greens with some shaved feta cheese and some pistachios. Drizzle some extra vinaigrette around each plate and serve. (Or serve family-style in a big bowl.)

mains

It was the main courses that determined that chapters in this book would be divided in two—Everyday Simple and Special Occasion.

The Everyday Simple mains include what I cook for my family during the week, after a busy workday. The rule is, it should take less than twenty minutes and use items already stocked in the fridge and pantry. Many of these recipes are family friendly and have two versions (like a herb risotto for the kids and a quick dress-up with pesto for the adults). Most of the Everyday Simple mains are one-pot dishes but can be simply and beautifully presented family-style for casual entertaining—like the Simple Thai Chicken Curry served in a large white bowl with an accompanying large bowl of rice, to be served and eaten in the kitchen or at the dining room table.

  The Special Occasion recipes are still straightforward, but a little more elegant, time consuming and even formal. These dishes are sure to impress guests and are great for a crowd, with simple finishes (like the cherry jus with the duck). They reveal fundamental restaurant techniques (like the steak au poivre, cooked stovetop over high heat and finished in the oven with a simple deglazed port reduction) that will leave your guests in awe!

EVERYDAY SIMPLE

chicken with sun-dried tomato cream

simple thai chicken curry

joshna's mom's chicken curry

balsamic pesto chicken

grilled butterflied leg of lamb for a crowd

pork tenderloin with grilled fruits

quick marinated flank steak

tandoori wild salmon

steamed mussels provençale

fresh spring pea risotto

pasta with arugula, mozzarella and roasted tomatoes

vegetarian pad thai

cheese fondue

creamed asparagus on toast

chicken with sun-dried tomato cream

This is not for the faint-hearted, but it's worth every calorie! My husband, Bryce, and I eat pasta all the time, and all these variations keep us from ever eating the same pasta twice, but we still keep coming back to this recipe. For a more substantial pasta, use spaghetti or penne. SERVES 4 TO 6

Mushrooms, tomatoes, artichokes or olives would be great additions to this dish. Variations include roasted red peppers and bacon—whatever inspires you from your pantry.

The cream can be reduced or even left out altogether. The flour and the starch in the pasta cooking water will thicken the sauce.

For a lighter, quicker preparation, leave out the flour. Use just the cream and the pasta water as thickeners.

INGREDIENTS

3 tbsp (50 mL) butter

1 tbsp (15 mL) olive oil

4 boneless skinless chicken breasts, cut crosswise in 1/2-inch (1 cm) strips

Salt and pepper, to taste

2 shallots, minced (about 1/4 cup/50 mL)

1/3 cup (75 mL) oil-packed sun-dried tomatoes, drained and finely chopped

2/3 cup (150 mL) 35% cream

1/2 cup (125 mL) dry white wine

3 tbsp (50 mL) fresh basil chiffonade

1 lb (500 g) spaghettini (thin spaghetti)

METHOD

Bring a large pot of salted water to a boil.

Meanwhile, melt butter and oil in a large sauté pan over medium-high heat. Season chicken with salt and pepper. Brown chicken until light gold and just cooked through (about 5 minutes); transfer to a plate.

Add shallots to pan and sauté for 1 minute. Add tomatoes, cream and wine. Bring to a boil and cook, stirring occasionally, until sauce thickens (about 4 minutes). Stir in basil and season with salt and pepper. Return chicken to sauce and simmer until heated through.

Cook pasta until al dente. Drain, reserving 1 cup (250 mL) pasta water. Stir pasta into sauce and add enough pasta water to thin sauce if necessary. Serve immediately.

To cut a chiffonade, stack herb (or vegetable) leaves, roll them up in a cigar shape and slice thinly. This technique makes a pretty garnish and avoids bruising tender leaves.

simple thai chicken curry

This recipe was my first attempt at making a segue into a simple Thai dish, and I still cook it often. Thai curries vary greatly in heat and flavour, so experiment. I like yellow curry paste for its slightly mellower flavour and heat. SERVES 6

Once you have the ingredients in your pantry, this takes no time to prepare.

Pork or beef would work well in this recipe.

Broccoli and firm tofu instead of chicken, and vegetable stock instead of chicken stock make a great vegetarian option.

INGREDIENTS

2 tsp (10 mL) vegetable oil

6 small boneless skinless chicken breasts, cut into strips lengthwise

1 tsp (5 mL) green or yellow curry paste *(or more to taste, if you want more heat)*

1/2 cup (125 mL) diced onion

2 shallots, diced

1/2 cup (125 mL) chicken stock

1 cup (250 mL) light coconut milk

2 tsp (10 mL) fish sauce

1 red bell pepper, thinly sliced

1 yellow bell pepper, thinly sliced

1/2 cup (125 mL) frozen baby peas

Leaves from 1 small bunch basil, cut in chiffonade

Salt, to taste

METHOD

Heat a sauté pan over medium-high heat. Add vegetable oil to hot pan. Quickly brown chicken strips (they do not need to be cooked through), then remove and set aside.

Stir in curry paste and cook briefly, stirring, until just turning brown (be careful not to burn it). Add onion and shallots; sauté until translucent. Add stock and stir to scrape up any brown bits. Add coconut milk and fish sauce; bring to a boil. Add chicken and peppers and cook until chicken is cooked through and peppers are tender, about 5 minutes.

Add frozen peas and cook an additional 2 minutes. Stir in basil and season with salt. Serve family-style over steaming jasmine rice.

joshna's mom's chicken curry

Joshna is one of our vibrant dish teachers and *party dish* chefs. She shared this family recipe at a class co-taught by her mom, and it was a huge success. Joshna's mother's kitchen has produced countless pots of this curry, and there are rarely leftovers. Adjust masala quantities to your taste. SERVES 4 TO 6

For more about garam masala, see tip on page 140.

DRIED HERBS AND SPICES
These are fresh and useable for only 6 months. If they have no smell and look like sawdust, pitch them! Hit your local bulk shop and buy small quantities of the freshest spices. It is best to buy your spices whole. Dry toast them in a small skillet and grind as you need them. Store them in a dark, cool place in an airtight container.

INGREDIENTS

3 tbsp (50 mL) vegetable oil or ghee
4 to 5 fresh or dried curry leaves
   (optional)
1 to 2 fresh whole green chilies, split in
   half lengthwise
1 tsp (5 mL) cumin seeds
2 yellow cooking onions, finely chopped
2 tbsp (25 mL) minced garlic
1 tsp (5 mL) minced fresh ginger
2 tsp (10 mL) ground cumin

1 tsp (5 mL) cayenne, or to taste
1 tsp (5 mL) ground coriander
1/2 tsp (2 mL) turmeric
Kosher salt, to taste
2 to 3 lb (1 to 1.5 kg) boneless skinless
   chicken (a mix of thighs and breasts)
1 1/2 cups (375 mL) puréed tomatoes
1 tbsp (15 mL) garam masala
Finely chopped fresh cilantro, for
   garnish

METHOD

In a large, heavy saucepan, heat oil over high heat. Standing back, add curry leaves, green chilies and cumin seeds—watch out, because they will splutter—and fry for about 1 minute. Add onions and fry for about 4 minutes, until they turn a rich golden brown but do not burn. Reduce heat to medium.

Add garlic and ginger and cook, stirring frequently, until light brown, 2 to 3 minutes. Add cumin, cayenne, coriander, turmeric and salt. Cook 1 to 2 minutes to heat and combine spices.

Increase heat to medium-high and add chicken pieces. Toss to coat with onions and spices, and fry for about 5 minutes or until chicken is well coated in the spices and lightly browned. Remove chilies and curry leaves.

Add tomatoes and stir well. Bring to a boil. Reduce heat to low and simmer, uncovered, for about 20 minutes or until chicken is well cooked. Sprinkle in garam masala, cover and continue to simmer for 10 to 15 minutes to allow flavours to blend. Serve hot, garnished with cilantro.

balsamic pesto chicken

This is one of my best go-to simple mid-week dinners. All you need is a couple of pantry essentials: balsamic vinegar and pesto. Slice the chicken thinly on an angle for a simple, pretty presentation. SERVES 6

Serve this chicken over garlic-butter spaghetti and the kids will gobble it up.

Alternatively, you can barbecue the chicken till cooked through and nicely grill-marked, about 15 minutes.

INGREDIENTS

Chicken
1/2 cup (125 mL) pesto *(see below or use store-bought)*
1 cup (250 mL) balsamic vinegar
1/2 cup (125 mL) olive oil
Kosher salt and freshly ground pepper, to taste
6 boneless chicken breasts, skin on

Classic Pesto
2 1/2 cups (625 mL) basil leaves
1/4 cup (50 mL) pine nuts, toasted
1 clove garlic
Salt, to taste
1/4 tsp (1 mL) freshly ground pepper
3/4 cup (175 mL) olive oil
1/2 cup (125 mL) freshly grated Parmesan cheese *(optional)*

METHOD

To make Classic Pesto, place basil, pine nuts, garlic, salt and pepper in bowl of food processor. Pulse a few times just to mix. While motor is running, slowly add enough olive oil to form a paste. Stir in Parmesan, if desired.

Whisk together pesto, vinegar, oil, salt and pepper in a large nonaluminum bowl. Add chicken and turn to coat. Marinate, covered and refrigerated, at least 2 hours or overnight.

Preheat oven to 400°F (200°C). Place chicken and marinade in a casserole dish and bake for 20 to 25 minutes or until juices run clear when chicken is pierced.

grilled butterflied leg of lamb for a crowd

When my brother Tim was in high school, he took gourmet cooking classes from the headmaster's wife, who provided some outstanding recipes that our family still uses today. This one is a staple in our house. Ask your butcher to butterfly the lamb to a consistent thickness for even cooking. This is so flavourful on its own, or wonderful with our Mint Pesto (page 164), minted yogurt or Tzatziki *(recipe at right)*. SERVES 8

INGREDIENTS

1/3 cup (75 mL) honey
1/4 cup (50 mL) vegetable oil
3 tbsp (50 mL) Dijon mustard
1 tbsp (15 mL) whole or roughly chopped fresh rosemary
Juice of 1 lemon
1 small onion, chopped
2 cloves garlic, minced
Salt and pepper, to taste
5 lb (2.2 kg) boneless butterflied leg of lamb
Lemon wedges

METHOD

Combine honey, oil, mustard, rosemary, lemon juice, onion, garlic, salt and pepper in a bowl. Pour into a resealable freezer bag. Add lamb, seal bag and shake to coat lamb. Marinate, refrigerated, overnight or up to 2 days. When ready to cook, remove lamb from bag and discard marinade. Remove any of the remaining ingredients from the lamb (or they'll burn when the meat is searing).

Preheat grill to high. Sear lamb fat-side down until a crust forms (about 10 minutes). Flip lamb. Reduce heat to medium and cook for another 20 minutes or until meat thermometer reads 135 to 140°F (58 to 60°C) for medium-rare. Let rest 10 minutes before slicing.

tzatziki

MAKES 2 CUPS (500 ML)

INGREDIENTS

3 cups (750 mL) full-fat yogurt
1 small English cucumber
1 to 2 cloves garlic, finely minced
1 tbsp (15 mL) lemon juice
Salt and pepper, to taste

METHOD

Place yogurt in a medium bowl. Coarsely grate cucumber. Place in a clean tea towel or paper towel and twist to squeeze out as much liquid as possible. Add cucumber to yogurt. Add garlic and lemon juice; stir together well. Season generously with salt and pepper.

Serve lamb with tzatziki and lemon wedges.

pork tenderloin with grilled fruits

Our son, Findlay, is a picky eater, but he loves helping to make this dish by sprinkling and testing my dad's maple syrup along the way. When the kids get involved in the cooking, they are much more inclined to dig in and truly enjoy. Even Olivia as a toddler devours this dish. This pork is wonderful served with sweet potato mash or fries. SERVES 6

GARAM MASALA—the name means warm spices—is an Indian blend of ground roasted spices. Mixes vary but typically contain cumin, coriander, pepper, cloves, cinnamon and cardamom. Look for it in specialty food shops and use with chicken and pork. Buy in small portions and store in a cool, dark place for no more than 6 months.

For a one-dish wonder, top small slices of sweet potato and these fruits with butter, brown sugar and curry powder and bake for 30 minutes.

INGREDIENTS

2 pork tenderloins (about 3/4 lb/375 g each)
1 golden pineapple, peeled, cored and sliced in 1-inch (2.5 cm) rings
3 ripe peaches, pitted and cut in half
1 tbsp (15 mL) butter, softened

Rub
2 tbsp (25 mL) garam masala
2 tbsp (25 mL) kosher salt
1 tbsp (15 mL) pepper
1/4 cup (50 mL) maple syrup
2 tbsp (25 mL) vegetable oil
2 tbsp (25 mL) Dijon mustard

METHOD

Mix rub ingredients together. Rub onto tenderloins and marinate, covered and refrigerated, for at least 1 hour and up to 6 hours.

Preheat barbecue to medium-high. Lightly brush fruit with butter and grill pork and fruit for 10 to 15 minutes or until internal temperature of pork reaches 145 to 150°F (65°C) and fruit is soft.

Let pork rest 10 minutes before slicing. Serve with grilled fruits.

everyday simple | mains

ALTERNATIVELY, YOU CAN
OVEN ROAST THIS DISH:

Preheat oven to 400°F (200°C).
Heat an oven-proof skillet over
high heat until very hot; add oil.
Season pork with salt and pepper.
Sear pork on all sides for 2 to
3 minutes, until a golden crust is
created. Remove to a plate.

Cover tenderloins with mustard,
garam masala and maple syrup on
all sides. Return to skillet and bake
for 12 to 15 minutes, until cooked
through but slightly pink in the
middle—or until a meat thermometer reads 150°F (65°C).

Once pork is in oven, lightly brush
fruits with butter, place on a baking sheet and roast in oven until
soft and golden, about 20 minutes.

Let pork rest 10 minutes before
slicing thinly. Serve with oven-
roasted fruits.

quick marinated flank steak

When my friend Tori phones from London with a cooking 911 call, I remind her of this marinade: 1/3, 1/3, 1/3 . . . all you need to remember is it's red wine, not red wine vinegar! This is definitely a mid-week staple of ours, but it doubles as the perfect no-stress casual entertaining dish.
SERVES 4

Delicious served with Sautéed Winter Greens or Spicy Broccolini (pages 190-191). For an Asian twist, add a few pieces of fresh ginger to the marinade and serve with sesame broccoli.

INGREDIENTS
2 lb (1 kg) flank steak

Marinade
1/3 cup (75 mL) red wine
1/3 cup (75 mL) olive oil
1/3 cup (75 mL) soy sauce
1 red onion, diced
2 cloves garlic, smashed

METHOD
Score steak partway through in a criss-cross pattern. In a nonaluminum bowl, mix red wine, olive oil and soy sauce. Transfer to a resealable plastic bag. Add onions, garlic and steak. Shake bag to coat steak with marinade and marinate, refrigerated, overnight or up to 24 hours, turning occasionally.
Preheat grill to high. Remove steak from marinade and discard marinade. Grill steak to desired doneness, 5 to 7 minutes per side for medium-rare. Let rest 10 minutes, tented with foil. Slice thinly across the grain.

tandoori wild salmon

Tandoori is a cooking style used throughout India. The word comes from the traditional rounded tandoor oven made of brick and clay and used to cook foods directly over a smoky fire. Chicken and fish cooked with this method are called tandoori. Tandoori spices are sold in powder and paste forms so those outside India can capture a bit of its incredible flavour. Try this with chicken breasts as a variation with mint raita. SERVES 6

INGREDIENTS
6 wild salmon fillets (each 1 inch/2.5 cm and 6 oz/175 g)

Marinade
6 tbsp (90 mL) tandoori powder
1/2 cup (125 mL) canola oil
1/2 cup (125 mL) fresh lime juice
1/4 cup (50 mL) cilantro, chopped
1 tbsp (15 mL) each minced garlic, shallots and ginger

METHOD
Pat salmon dry. Place in a dish just large enough to hold it. To make the marinade, in a food processor, combine tandoori powder, oil, lime juice, cilantro, garlic, shallots and ginger. Process until smooth. Pour marinade over salmon, covering completely. Marinate salmon, covered and refrigerated, for 3 hours.

Lightly oil grill and preheat to medium-high. Remove salmon from marinade; gently scrape marinade off salmon and reserve marinade.

Grill salmon 2 minutes, then give fillets a quarter turn and grill 2 minutes more to create a criss-cross of grill marks. Carefully turn salmon and grill about 2 minutes more, or until cooked through. Brush with reserved marinade a few minutes before salmon is cooked.

Preheat oven to 400°F (200°C). Remove salmon from marinade; gently scrape marinade off salmon. Place salmon on a parchment-lined baking sheet and bake for 8 minutes, or until the middle is just set.

Serve the salmon with Mango Salsa (page 64), if you like, or try serving with a delicious Lime Coconut Butter Sauce:

Bring 3 tbsp (50 mL) 35% cream, 2 tbsp (25 mL) coconut milk and 1 tbsp (15 mL) fresh lime juice to a simmer. Remove from heat and whisk in 3 tbsp (50 mL) cold, unsalted butter, cubed, one piece at a time. Season and sprinkle with some chopped green onion.

Here is an easy oven method if it's too cold to grill: Preheat oven to 400°F (200°C). Remove salmon from marinade; gently scrape marinade off salmon. Place salmon on a parchment-lined baking sheet and bake for 8 minutes, or until the middle is just set.

steamed mussels provençale

I like to include mussels on the menu when I'm teaching a Provençale class. Mussels are simple to prepare at home, and are surprisingly inexpensive. This recipe demystifies mussels; all you need to remember is to buy them fresh from a reputable fishmonger and eat them the same day. SERVES 4

For a lighter, more authentic Provençale version, leave out the cream and include some olives and capers. For a wonderful Thai version, cook some green curry paste with the onions and use coconut milk instead of the cream. This is also great as an appetizer with a good bottle of wine.

INGREDIENTS

2 lb (1 kg) mussels
2 tbsp (25 mL) olive oil
2 large shallots, diced
2 cloves garlic, minced
1 can (28 oz/796 mL) diced tomatoes, drained
1 cup (250 mL) white wine
1 cup (250 mL) 35% cream
Salt and pepper, to taste
2 tbsp (25 mL) chopped fresh thyme

METHOD

Scrub mussels, removing beards. Discard any that do not close when tapped and those that are cracked. Set aside.

In a large saucepan or Dutch oven, heat oil over medium heat. Add shallots and garlic; cook, stirring frequently, until fragrant and tender (about 4 minutes). Add diced tomatoes and bring to a boil, stirring for 3 to 5 minutes. Add white wine and cook for another 5 minutes. Add cream and reduce until it thickens enough to coat the back of the spoon. Season with salt and pepper.

Add mussels and thyme. Steam, covered, for 3 to 5 minutes, until mussels open up. Discard any unopened mussels. Spoon mussels and sauce into serving bowls and serve with crusty bread to mop up the sauce.

fresh spring pea risotto

This recipe is a template for you to use as a guide. It reveals the key techniques for a successful risotto. Once you're comfortable with risotto, try our variations or use your imagination. As passionate Italian chef in Toronto and dish teacher Massimo Capra preaches, cook with your heart! (And with a glass of wine in the other hand!)

SERVES 4 TO 6

A FEW KEY TIPS

Use only best-quality ingredients—Carnaroli or Vialone Nano rice, good Parmesan, good stock.

Use a wide, shallow, heavy-bottomed sauté pan so the rice grains cook evenly—risotto should be only one storey high!

The ideal rice-to-liquid ratio is 1 to 3 or 4.

Keep the stock hot and keep the heat under the risotto high enough that you can see bubbles around the edge. More liquid must be added before the risotto goes dry.

Serve immediately so the risotto is still creamy.

INGREDIENTS

5 cups (1.25 L) stock *(vegetable or chicken, preferably homemade)*
3 tbsp (50 mL) olive oil
1/3 cup (75 mL) plus 2 tbsp (25 mL) butter
2 medium onions, finely chopped
2 cloves garlic, finely chopped
Kosher salt and freshly ground black pepper, to taste
1 1/2 cups (375 mL) Carnaroli, Vialone Nano or Arborio rice
1 cup (250 mL) dry white wine
1 cup (250 mL) fresh peas or frozen petits pois
1 cup (250 mL) freshly grated Parmesan cheese

METHOD

Heat stock in a saucepan; keep stock at a gentle simmer.

In a large sauté pan, heat olive oil and 2 tbsp (25 mL) butter over medium heat; add the onions and cook, stirring often, until softened (about 7 minutes). Add garlic and cook for a few minutes more. Season with salt and pepper.

Stir in rice. Let rice fry a bit with the onions, stirring often. After a minute the rice will look slightly translucent. Add wine and cook, stirring, until wine is absorbed.

Add your first ladle (about 1/2 cup/125 mL) of hot stock. Turn down the heat to a brisk simmer so the rice doesn't cook too quickly on the outside. Stir until almost all the stock is absorbed (don't let rice go dry), then add another ladle of stock, stirring until each addition is absorbed before adding more, until rice is soft but has a slight bite. This will take 17 to 20 minutes. When risotto is almost done, add fresh peas and cook for 3 minutes more (frozen peas need only 1 to 2 minutes). When peas are tender and risotto is al dente, remove pan from the heat.

Quickly stir in remaining 1/3 cup (75 mL) butter and Parmesan. Season, and serve.

variations

asparagus risotto

Remove woody ends from asparagus. Cut stems and tips into bite-size pieces. Add 3 minutes before cooking is completed. Finish as for main recipe.

risotto verde

Stir in herb pesto halfway through cooking. In the last minute, stir in chopped fresh parsley. Finish as for main recipe.

mushroom risotto

Add 1 1/2 cups (375 mL) chopped assorted mushrooms (*cremini, oyster, shiitake*) after onions are sautéed. Finish as for main recipe.

beet risotto *(pictured at left)*

Wash, peel and cook 3 medium beets in 5 cups (1.25 L) water or stock until beets are tender (30 to 40 minutes). Reserve beet stock and use as risotto liquid. Cool beets, grate and set aside. After wine is absorbed, begin adding beet liquid as above. Halfway through cooking, add grated beets. Finish as for main recipe.

risotto alla milanese

Add a few pinches of saffron threads to your simmering stock. It will turn the risotto a gorgeous deep yellow colour. Stir in some fresh orange zest and the juice of 2 oranges at the end with the butter and Parmesan.

pasta with arugula, mozzarella and roasted tomatoes

Pasta is something I cook at least once a week, and rarely from a recipe. This rustic warm pasta salad is one of Sacha's most popular pasta dishes from her "Naked in Italy" classes. Let this recipe act as a canvas for you to be creative. It's really about stocking the pantry with pasta, olives, capers, roasted red peppers, sun-dried tomatoes and oil. Then stock the fridge with onions, garlic, cheeses, creams, pesto, greens and fresh vegetables. No two pastas are the same. Be an artist and interpret as you will. SERVES 6 TO 8

For a quick fix, replace roasted tomatoes with chopped drained oil-packed sun-dried tomatoes. Also great with roasted red peppers.

Always reserve some pasta water to add at the end, if necessary, to give your sauced pasta the desired consistency. Never rinse your pasta.

Pasta looks best served in an oversized flat soup bowl or on a charger plate. Using tongs, mound pasta in the middle of the plate, twisting it tightly to give the mound some height.

INGREDIENTS

6 tbsp (90 mL) pesto (page 138 or use store-bought, optional)
2 tbsp (25 mL) olive oil, plus more for serving
2 large balls fior di latte or buffalo mozzarella (or 1/2 cup/125 mL crumbled feta)
2 bunches arugula, tough stems removed
1/4 cup (50 mL) balsamic vinegar
1 lb (500 g) dried spaghetti
1/2 cup (125 mL) freshly grated Parmesan cheese
18 roasted tomato halves *(opposite)* or Slow-roasted Tomatoes (page 189)
Salt and pepper

METHOD

Thin pesto with olive oil and set aside. Cut or tear fior di latte into smaller pieces and set aside. Dress arugula with balsamic vinegar and set aside.

Cook pasta in a large pot of boiling salted water until al dente. Reserve 1/2 cup (125 mL) pasta water. Drain pasta and immediately transfer it to a large bowl while there are still drops of water adhering to it. Toss pasta with pesto to give a uniform thin coating, then add arugula, grated Parmesan and fior di latte. Gently toss again and season to taste. Add some of the reserved pasta water if necessary to get the desired creamy consistency.

Mound pasta on plates and top with roasted tomatoes. Drizzle with some more olive oil. Finish with more ground pepper.

roasted tomatoes

INGREDIENTS
9 ripe plum tomatoes
1/4 cup (50 mL) olive oil
1/4 cup (50 mL) balsamic vinegar
Salt and pepper

METHOD
Preheat oven to 450°F (230°C). Cut out the stem end of the tomatoes and slice
tomatoes in half lengthwise. Place cut side up on a baking sheet. Drizzle with
olive oil and balsamic vinegar. Salt and pepper lightly. Roast for 20 minutes or
until tomatoes are soft. Let cool.

vegetarian pad thai

Pad Thai is one of those cravings, one of those dishes you usually go out for or order in . . . but you can make it at home, and it's a great (and inexpensive) way to satisfy a crowd. Stock your pantry with Thai essentials and the rest is easy. Leftovers reheat well. SERVES 4 TO 6

INGREDIENTS

Stir-fry
1/2 lb (250 g) rice stick noodles
2 tbsp (25 mL) vegetable oil
2 cloves garlic, finely chopped
2 eggs, lightly beaten
2 cups (500 mL) bean sprouts,
  washed and drained
1/4 cup (50 mL) coarsely chopped
  peanuts
4 green onions, cut in 1/2-inch (1 cm)
  pieces
1 red pepper, very thinly sliced
1/2 cup (125 mL) homemade Peanut
  Sauce *(see recipe opposite) (optional)*

Sauce
1/2 cup (125 mL) puréed tomatoes
1/2 cup (125 mL) Thai fish sauce
1/2 cup (125 mL) sugar
1/4 cup (50 mL) lime juice,
  or more to taste
2 tsp (10 mL) dried chili flakes,
  or to taste

Garnish
1/4 cup (50 mL) coarsely chopped
  peanuts
1 lemon, cut in wedges
1/4 cup (50 mL) chopped fresh cilantro

METHOD

Soak rice noodles in very warm water for 30 minutes, until soft. Drain just before using.

To make the sauce, in a small bowl, mix together puréed tomatoes, fish sauce, sugar, lime juice and chili flakes. Set aside.

In a large wok over high heat, heat oil. Cook garlic for 3 minutes, until brown. Add drained (but still wet) noodles. Add eggs and toss continuously until noodles are coated and eggs are set (about 2 minutes). Add fish sauce mixture. Stir-fry for about 3 minutes or until sauce is combined. Add bean sprouts, peanuts, green onions, red pepper and Peanut Sauce. Stir-fry for 2 minutes.

Serve immediately, garnished with chopped peanuts, lemon wedges and cilantro.

peanut sauce

This sauce is also great served with shrimp chips and as a marinade and dip for chicken satays.

MAKES ABOUT 1 1/2 CUPS (375 ML)

INGREDIENTS

1 1/2 tsp (7 mL) vegetable oil
1 clove garlic, crushed
1 tsp (5 mL) red curry paste
  or chili sambal
1/2 can (14 oz/398 mL)
  coconut milk *(not low fat)*
2 tbsp (25 mL) sugar
2 tbsp (25 mL) lemon juice
1 cup (250 mL) ground peanuts
Salt and pepper, to taste

METHOD

In a small saucepan, heat oil over
  medium heat. Cook garlic, stirring,
  until just golden. Add curry paste
  and continue stirring for 2 minutes.
  Add coconut milk and sugar. Bring
  to a boil, reduce heat to medium
  and simmer 10 minutes.
Add lemon juice and ground peanuts.
  Continue cooking, stirring, until
  sauce is combined and thick.
  Remove from heat, season with salt
  and pepper, and let cool.

cheese fondue

We had a cheese fondue party in one of the *party dish* episodes with good friends as guests. A relic of the '70s, fondue proved to be wonderful food for an interactive family-style dinner party. SERVES 6

Serve fondue with an assortment of dippers like a variety of good breads (brioche, baguette, crusty sourdough, raisin-walnut, whole grain) cut into bite-size pieces, fruits (apples, pears, figs) and vegetables (blanched asparagus, cauliflower, new potatoes, green beans and raw cherry tomatoes).

INGREDIENTS

1 clove garlic, halved crosswise
1 1/2 cups (375 mL) dry white wine
2 tbsp (25 mL) brandy
1 tbsp (15 mL) kirsch
1 tbsp (15 mL) cornstarch
1/2 lb (250 g) Emmental cheese, coarsely shredded *(2 cups/500 mL)*
1/2 lb (250 g) Gruyère cheese, coarsely shredded *(2 cups/500 mL)*

METHOD

Rub inside of a 4-quart (4 L) heavy saucepan with cut sides of garlic, then discard garlic. Add wine to pot and bring just to a simmer over medium heat.

In a small bowl, stir together brandy, kirsch and cornstarch. Set aside.

Gradually add cheeses to pot and cook, stirring constantly in a zigzag pattern (not a circular motion) to prevent cheese from balling up, until cheese is just melted and creamy (do not let it boil). Stir cornstarch mixture again and stir into fondue. Bring fondue to a simmer and cook, stirring, until thickened, 5 to 8 minutes.

Transfer to a fondue pot set over a flame and serve with dippers.

creamed asparagus on toast

I've modified one of my grandmother's favourite springtime light supper dishes with an extra-rich cheese sauce. SERVES 4

INGREDIENTS

2 tbsp (25 mL) butter

2 tbsp (25 mL) all-purpose flour

2/3 cup (150 mL) warm milk

1/4 cup (50 mL) shredded sharp Cheddar or grated Parmesan cheese *(optional)*

1/2 tsp (2 mL) dry mustard

A pinch of cayenne pepper

16 asparagus spears, woody ends trimmed

4 slices hot buttered toast

METHOD

In a small saucepan over medium-low heat, melt butter. Add flour and cook, stirring, for 2 minutes. Slowly whisk in milk and cook, whisking constantly, for 3 minutes. Remove from heat and stir in cheese (if using), mustard and cayenne. Set aside, keeping warm.

Steam asparagus on a steaming rack until tender-crisp. Stir asparagus into cheese sauce and spoon onto hot buttered toast.

SPECIAL OCCASIONS

---

no-fail roast chicken

seared duck breast with sour cherries and port

herb-crusted beef tenderloin

steak au poivre with port reduction and horseradish aïoli

latin-spiced beef with smoky tomato relish

rack of lamb with mint pesto

wild salmon niçoise

pan-seared scallops with leek and tarragon sauce

grilled calamari with tomato olive salsa

no-fail roast chicken

A roast chicken is a special-occasion family favourite at my mom's and grandmother's tables. They make a more traditional (and time-consuming) gravy from the drippings. This is a simpler version for the time-pressed family. SERVES 4

INGREDIENTS

1 roasting chicken *(3 lb/1.5 kg)*, rinsed and patted dry
Kosher salt and pepper, to taste
2 or 3 sprigs rosemary or thyme
1 head garlic, halved
1/2 onion
1 lemon, quartered
1 to 2 tbsp (15 to 25 mL) plus 1 tbsp (15 mL) butter
1/4 cup (50 mL) white wine
1 cup (250 mL) chicken stock

METHOD

Preheat oven to 400°F (200°C). Sprinkle chicken cavity liberally with salt and pepper. Place herbs, garlic, onion and lemon in cavity. Rub chicken all over with 1 to 2 tbsp (15 to 25 mL) butter. Sprinkle liberally with salt and pepper.

Place chicken in a roasting pan or 12-inch (30 cm) cast-iron frying pan. Roast, uncovered, basting several times, until chicken is cooked (a good hour). Juices should run clear, and a sharp knife inserted between the thigh and the breast should come out hot; a meat thermometer inserted in the thigh, closest to the body, should read 170°F (75°C). Transfer chicken to cutting board and tent loosely with foil. Let sit while you make the sauce.

Place roasting pan over medium heat (you may need to use two burners). Add wine and scrape up the bits from the bottom. Turn up heat and add chicken stock. Boil until reduced by half. Season with salt and pepper and stir in remaining 1 tbsp (15 mL) of butter. Simmer a few minutes until the desired thickness.

Cut wings and legs from chicken; cut legs in half if desired. Remove breast meat in one piece, then slice. Arrange chicken on a serving plate and glaze with sauce. Serve immediately.

seared duck breast with sour cherries and port

My first experience with cooking duck was catering for author Maeve Binchy. Uncertain how to crisp up the intimidating layer of fat on the duck, I called my grandmother, who explained the importance of rendering all of the fat, leaving only a very thin layer of delicious, crispy skin. SERVES 6

INGREDIENTS

2 1/2 lb (1.25 kg) duck breasts *(about 3 breasts)*, fat scored

Salt and pepper, to taste

3 shallots, minced

2 cloves garlic, minced

1 cup (250 mL) port

1/2 cup (125 mL) maple syrup

1/4 cup (50 mL) balsamic vinegar

3 Granny Smith apples, cored and cut into 1/2-inch (1 cm) cubes

1 1/2 cups (375 mL) sour cherries, pitted

2 tsp (10 mL) finely chopped fresh thyme *(or 1 tsp/5 mL finely chopped fresh sage)*

METHOD

Preheat oven to 450°F (230°C). Heat a large skillet over medium heat. Sear breasts, fat-side down, for 10 to 20 minutes or until skin is browned and crispy (the fat will start to turn to liquid in the pan). Remove from heat. Transfer duck to a small roasting pan. Carefully drain all but 2 tbsp (25 mL) duck fat from skillet.

Season duck on both sides with salt and pepper. Roast, skin side up, for 7 to 10 minutes or until medium-rare (a meat thermometer will read 125 to 130°F/ 50 to 55°C). Remove from oven and let rest 10 minutes.

Meanwhile, in same skillet over medium heat, sauté shallots in duck fat until translucent (about 2 minutes). Add garlic and sauté until fragrant (about 1 minute). Add port, maple syrup and balsamic vinegar; cook, scraping bottom of pan, until liquid is reduced by half. Add apples, cherries and thyme; cook until apples are tender but still maintain colour and shape (about 3 minutes).

Slice duck breast thinly across the grain. Serve with sour cherry sauce.

Because duck is so high in fat, cooking it creates a lot of smoke. Make sure your fan is on high and the door or window open! Sear the breasts ahead of time so the air can clear before your guests arrive. You can hold the seared duck for up to 1 hour at room temperature. Finish in the oven while guests are enjoying their appetizers.

A somewhat less smoky cooking method is to start the duck in a cold pan. Bring the temperature slowly up to medium to gradually render the fat and brown the skin.

Don't overcook the apples—you want to maintain their shape and green colour. You can also thinly slice the apples instead and fan them out on the plate.

You can also use large dried cherries, figs or cranberries, but you'll need to cook them a little longer than fresh ones. When in season, use fresh cherries.

herb-crusted beef tenderloin

This recipe has been my staple "elegant main" in cooking classes taught throughout the years. The original recipe involved searing, crusting and finishing in the oven. But just as delicious, faster and easier on the cleanup is this one-step in-the-oven method. SERVES 6 TO 8

Onions should be blanched and peeled 1 day ahead; they are a bit finicky. Cover and refrigerate.

My favourite combo in the winter is to serve this with our White Vegetable Purée (page 193) and wilted spinach.

INGREDIENTS

1 beef tenderloin, centre cut only *(2 to 3 lb/1 to 1.5 kg)*
Salt and pepper, to taste
2 tbsp (25 mL) Dijon mustard
1/4 cup (50 mL) each chopped fresh thyme, rosemary and Italian parsley

Sauce

1 bag (10 oz/284 g) fresh pearl onions
2 cups (500 mL) balsamic vinegar
1/4 cup (50 mL) honey

METHOD

Preheat oven to 500°F (260°C). Place meat in a roasting pan and season generously with salt and pepper. Rub meat with Dijon mustard, then coat all sides with the herbs. Roast for 20 minutes or until a meat thermometer reads 125°F (50°C) for rare, 135°F (58°C) for medium-rare. Remove from oven and let rest 10 minutes before slicing thinly.

While beef is roasting, make the sauce. Cook pearl onions in a large pot of boiling salted water 2 minutes; drain. Trim root ends, leaving base intact. Remove outer skins when cool enough to handle.

In a medium saucepan over medium-high heat, reduce balsamic vinegar and honey by half (10 to 15 minutes). Season with salt and pepper. Add pearl onions; cook for a few minutes more until onions are tender and warmed through. Drizzle sauce over sliced meat.

This beef tenderloin is a delicious main served to a hungry crowd at a buffet. Serve with pearl onions or caramelized onions, and Horseradish Aïoli (page 160). It's just as good at room temperature, so cook it before your guests arrive and don't worry about serving it piping hot.

rack of lamb with mint pesto

Elegant and impressive, this dish is a classic beauty. It was my first photographed dish to appear in a magazine, and is still my food-styling favourite. To serve, put the chops on the plate, loin down, leaning the bones upwards and criss-crossing them. Serve with our White Vegetable Purée (page 193) and wilted greens acting as anchors in the centre of the plate. To save time, ask your butcher to French the lamb. SERVES 6

Pesto can be made ahead and stored in the fridge for 2 days. Leftovers are great as a spread in a lamb sandwich. And mint is great for the digestion!

I love this with roasted potatoes (the crispier, the better!).

An alternative to the Mint Pesto is a fresh Tzatziki (page 139) or minted yogurt.

This lamb is also wonderful with a fresh herb crust (rosemary, mint and thyme) pressed into the fat side after searing, before it goes in the oven.

For an elegant cocktail party, serve individual chops as "lamb lollipops."

INGREDIENTS

Mint Pesto

1 cup (250 mL) tightly packed fresh mint leaves
1/2 cup (125 mL) pine nuts, toasted
1 clove garlic, minced
Juice of 1 small lemon
1/4 cup (50 mL) olive oil
Salt and pepper

2 Frenched racks of lamb *(about 2 lb/1 kg)*
Salt and pepper, to taste
3 tbsp (50 mL) canola or grapeseed oil

METHOD

To make the Mint Pesto, pulse mint, pine nuts and garlic in a food processor. Add lemon juice and drizzle in olive oil with the motor running. Season with salt and pepper to taste. Set aside.

Preheat oven to 450°F (230°C). Trim any excess fat from lamb. Make sure racks are dry—pat dry with paper towel if needed. Season generously with salt and pepper.

Heat a large, heavy skillet over high heat. Add oil. When oil is hot but not smoking, sear racks one at a time, turning once, until both sides are golden brown. Transfer to a baking sheet and roast for 15 minutes or until medium-rare (meat thermometer reads 135 to 140°F/58 to 60°C). Transfer to a cutting board and let rest for 10 minutes before slicing into chops.

wild salmon niçoise

This light meal is perfect for an afternoon party – delicious, colourful and beautiful. Present it on a large white platter and group all the items together so it looks bountiful. This is a very popular room-temperature dish—perfect for entertaining a crowd in summer. SERVES 6

For a lunch, use 3-oz (90 g) fillets. For a buffet, serve the salmon (without the veg) on a separate platter, drizzled with the vinaigrette.

Always use wild salmon if you can—the colour and flavour are much better than farmed salmon. You may need to go to a fishmonger for this.

INGREDIENTS

1 lb (500 g) small red new potatoes
1 lb (500 g) green beans, trimmed
6 fillets wild salmon *(each 5 oz/150 g)*
3 tbsp (50 mL) grapeseed oil
Salt and pepper, to taste
1 pint (500 mL) cherry or grape tomatoes, halved
1 cup (250 mL) niçoise olives

Red Wine Vinaigrette

1/4 cup (50 mL) red wine vinegar
1 tbsp (15 mL) Dijon mustard
1 shallot, diced
3/4 cup (175 mL) extra-virgin olive oil
Salt and pepper, to taste

METHOD

Place potatoes in a large pot of cold salted water. Bring to a boil, reduce heat and simmer until potatoes are just fork tender (about 10 minutes). Drain and set aside.

Refill pot with water, salt generously and bring to a boil. Have ready a bowl of ice water. Blanch beans for about 3 minutes, until tender-crisp. Drain beans and immediately transfer to bowl of ice water. When completely cool, drain and pat dry. Set aside.

To make the vinaigrette, in a bowl, whisk together vinegar, mustard and shallot. Gradually drizzle in olive oil, whisking to create an emulsion. Season with salt and pepper. Set aside.

Rub salmon fillets with 1 tbsp (15 mL) of the grapeseed oil. Season generously with salt and pepper. Heat a large, heavy skillet over high heat (if using nonstick, heat over medium-high only). Add remaining oil. When oil is hot but not smoking, add salmon fillets, skin side up. Sear for 3 to 4 minutes, until a golden-brown crust has formed. Carefully turn over and sear on the skin side for another 2 minutes, until salmon is just barely cooked through.

In separate bowls, toss potatoes and green beans with enough vinaigrette to coat. Arrange on plates with tomatoes, olives and salmon. Drizzle with vinaigrette and season with salt and pepper.

pan-seared scallops
with leek and tarragon sauce

I fell in love with scallops while guiding bike tours for Butterfield &
Robinson, first in Provence and then in Nova Scotia. The East Coast Digby
scallops are the most flavourful, but tiny and a little trickier to plate.
SERVES 6

When buying scallops, make sure
they are dry (ideally flat, in one
layer, not sitting in liquid) and
odourless. Ask the fishmonger
when they came in (and use within
24 hours of that time). Sometimes
they have a small white muscle
attached to their sides. Simply pull
this off and discard.

This is also wonderful served on
top of angel hair pasta tossed
with a little sauce and reserved
pasta water.

INGREDIENTS

18 medium sea scallops *(10/20 size)*
Salt and freshly cracked pepper, to
taste
2 to 4 tbsp (25 to 50 mL) canola or
grapeseed oil
Olive oil, to taste
Frisée lettuce or any other bitter
green, for garnish

Sauce

1 tbsp (15 mL) butter
2 shallots, sliced
2 leeks *(white and light green part
only)*, sliced
3 cloves garlic, finely minced
1/2 cup (125 mL) white wine
1/2 cup (125 mL) 35% cream
2 tbsp (25 mL) finely chopped
fresh tarragon
Salt and pepper, to taste

METHOD

Pat scallops dry with paper towel. Season with salt and freshly cracked pepper on
both sides. Heat a large, heavy skillet over high heat. Add enough oil to just coat
the bottom of the pan. Sear scallops for 1 to 2 minutes per side or until crisp and
golden and just cooked through (you may need to do this in batches). Transfer
scallops to a plate.

To make the sauce, in the same skillet over medium heat, melt butter with a dash
of olive oil. Cook shallots and leeks until fragrant (about 5 minutes). Add garlic
and cook for another 3 minutes. Add white wine and cook, stirring, until reduced
by half. Add cream and reduce by about half (until it lightly coats the back of a
spoon). Stir in tarragon and season with salt and pepper.

Lightly toss frisée with a pinch of salt and a little olive oil. Place greens in centre of plates
and top with 3 cooked scallops each. Drizzle with sauce and serve immediately.

grilled calamari with tomato olive salsa

This is a wonderful light supper when served with frisée lettuce tossed in vinaigrette, a perfect summer backyard dinner with a crisp white wine. SERVES 6

The acid in the lemon juice will start to "cook" your calamari after about half an hour (producing a ceviche), so don't leave in the marinade for too long.

This salsa is also delicious served on rustic bread or a baguette as a quick appetizer.

INGREDIENTS

Salsa
6 plum tomatoes, chopped
1 red onion, finely diced
1/2 cup (125 mL) chopped pitted
   kalamata olives
2 tbsp (25 mL) capers
2 tbsp (25 mL) chopped fresh basil
2 cloves garlic, finely minced
1 tbsp (15 mL) lemon zest
Salt and pepper, to taste

Calamari
12 fresh medium-sized calamari,
   cleaned (ask your fishmonger
   to do this!)
1/4 cup (50 mL) olive oil
Juice of 1 lemon
1/4 tsp (1 mL) dried chili flakes
Salt and pepper, to taste

METHOD

To make the salsa, in a nonaluminum bowl, stir together tomatoes, onion, olives, capers, basil, garlic and lemon zest. Season with salt and pepper. Set aside while cooking calamari.

Preheat grill to high (or use a grill pan).

Using a sharp knife, cut slits in each calamari tube at 1/2-inch (1 cm) intervals, but do not cut right through to separate into rings. In a nonaluminum bowl, combine olive oil, lemon juice, chili flakes, salt and pepper. Stir in calamari and marinate for only 5 to 10 minutes.

Grill calamari on hot grill for 2 to 3 minutes per side or until just cooked through (calamari will start to curl up). The tentacles will take about a minute longer. Transfer to a plate. Top calamari with salsa and serve.

sides

The Riverdale farmers' market is at the end of our street and runs 5 months of the year. When our son Findlay was one, he tasted his first raw carrot, pulled from a local farmer's field that morning—go figure, he loved it! Every Tuesday we look forward to discovering the new vegetable varieties and the kids love having their say in menu planning. The effect of being involved first hand in the shopping experience turns the pickiest eaters into converts.

Spring brings us asparagus (like these, pulled from my dad's garden) and leeks, summer presents sweet carrots, late summer boasts tomatoes and corn and the fall digs deep into the earth for beets and turnips. It's simple to let the seasons guide us and let the vegetables speak for themselves (with a bit of butter, salt and pepper!) These recipes are simple dress-ups to the farmers' pride and joy.

Balance, colour, texture and flavour are important to every meal, and the sides are what pull it all together (and often that comforting gratin on the side is the reason we order a dish in a restaurant!). Simple, colourful grilled leeks are sometimes all you need to accompany your chicken dish.

For mid-week cooking, most of us don't use recipes for our regular broccoli or carrot dishes, but these simple everyday sides give a quick twist to what we may already be doing. Tart pickled cucumbers hearken back to the good old days, the gratin Dauphinois and the slow-roasted tomatoes are classics and some newer discoveries like the cumin-lime butter dress up our summer corn. These sides have not been divided into everyday simple and special occasion—they can always be stars on the plate.

haricots verts with pine nut butter

Using haricots verts (thinner and longer than our North American green beans) renders this dish not only quick and flavourful but also quite elegant. Certainly local green beans are the perfect choice for a quick mid-week veg fix. SERVES 4

To dress up this dish, wilt chives in hot water and tie bunches of green beans with a chive.

Green beans are also wonderful served cold. Once cooled in the ice water, drain and pat dry. Replace the pine nut butter with a shallot vinaigrette and serve as a room-temperature salad.

INGREDIENTS

1 lb (500 g) green beans
2 tbsp (25 mL) butter
1/4 cup (50 mL) pine nuts
Freshly grated black pepper, to taste

METHOD

Preheat oven to 350°F (180°C). Clean beans and trim stem ends. Have ready a bowl of ice water. Bring a medium pot of salted water to a boil. Boil beans until just tender but still crunchy, 3 to 5 minutes. Drain beans and immediately immerse in ice water to stop the cooking.

In a medium skillet over low heat, melt butter. Add pine nuts and cook, stirring occasionally, until nuts and butter are golden (about 5 minutes).

Place beans in a baking dish. Pour pine nut butter over beans and sprinkle with pepper. Bake, uncovered, until warm, 5 to 7 minutes. Serve immediately.

brown sugar carrots

It's amazing what a bit of brown sugar can do. With a very light dusting of sugar on carrots, our kids happily gobble up their vegetable quota. Adults love these carrots too, and if you cut them into pretty, uniform matchsticks, they dress up a plate nicely. SERVES 6

INGREDIENTS

2 bunches carrots *(with greens still on; don't use the kind in plastic bags)*
2 tbsp (25 mL) butter *(or to taste)*
1 tbsp (15 mL) brown sugar *(or to taste)*
Salt and pepper, to taste

METHOD

Peel carrots and slice into matchsticks. In a medium saucepan, bring water to a boil. Salt the water. Cook carrots until tender-crisp (about 5 minutes). Drain and put back into the warm pot. Stir in butter, sugar, salt and pepper and serve immediately.

It's not worth buying those lacklustre, flavourless baby carrots cleaned and ready to go in a bag. The real things take no time to peel. Local organic carrots taste best. Peel and cut uniformly, and store in a square glass vase in water in the fridge. They keep for days, are easy to pull out for a quick snack and can even decorate a table!

gratin of butternut squash

This is a rich side; a small portion will go a long way. A casual oven-to-table dish, this is intenstified with smoked cheese. SERVES 6 TO 8

Scamorza is a firm, slightly salty mozzarella cheese. Have fun and try other cheeses (but choose ones that melt well!) like smoked Gouda. Visit your local cheese shop and ask to test some new cheeses. This is a very rich dish, so pace yourself!

As an alternative to boiling the squash, you could roast it first, as pictured here. The roast squash is a delicious side dish on its own. Doctor it up with your favourite herbs and spices.

INGREDIENTS

1 large butternut squash (2 1/2 lb/1.25 kg), peeled and seeded
1 1/4 cups (300 mL) 35% cream
1/2 lb (250 g) smoked scamorza or smoked Gouda cheese, cut into about 6 slices
Salt and pepper, to taste

METHOD

Preheat oven to 400°F (200°C). Slice squash crosswise 1/4 inch (0.5 cm) thick using a food processor fitted with the slicing blade or a mandoline. (You could also slice by hand, but make sure that all the pieces are the same size or they will not cook evenly.)

Put squash slices in a large saucepan and cover with water. Bring to a boil over high heat and boil for 1 to 2 minutes or until slightly softened. Drain.

Arrange slices in a baking or gratin dish. Season with salt and pepper. Pour cream over squash and stir gently to distribute cream. Cover with cheese. Cover dish with foil and bake for 20 to 30 minutes or until squash is softened. Remove foil and place under broiler to brown the top. Serve immediately.

zucchini gratin

This is a mainstay from my cooking classes. I adapted it from one of my favourite cookbooks, Ina Garten's *Barefoot Contessa in Paris*. This is a wonderful winter vegetarian main. Adding flour and milk is a quicker way to create a sauce than making a separate béchamel.

SERVES 6

Secrets to pulling off a perfect gratin include sautéeing your aromatics (such as onions), adding flavourful liquids (cider, booze, stock) and giving crunch to your topping (bread crumbs, butter and more cheese!).

I like to keep Japanese panko bread crumbs stocked in the pantry—light and crispy, they are perfect for gratins, coating chicken or fish or giving texture to pastas.

INGREDIENTS

3 tbsp (50 mL) plus 1 tbsp (15 mL) butter

2 large yellow onions, sliced

4 to 5 zucchini, sliced 1/4 inch (0.5 cm) thick

1 1/2 tsp (7 mL) salt

1 tsp (5 mL) pepper

1/4 tsp (1 mL) grated nutmeg

2 tbsp (25 mL) all-purpose flour

1 cup (250 mL) hot milk

3/4 cup (175 mL) panko bread crumbs

3/4 cup (175 mL) grated Gruyère cheese

METHOD

Preheat oven to 400°F (200°C). Melt 3 tbsp (50 mL) of the butter in a large sauté pan over medium-low heat. Cook onions, stirring occasionally, until tender (about 15 minutes). Add zucchini, salt, pepper and nutmeg; cook, covered, until zucchini is slightly tender but not mushy (5 minutes). Gently stir in flour, being careful not to break up zucchini. Add hot milk, reduce heat to low and cook until milk thickens and makes a sauce. Carefully pour into a 13- x 9-inch (3 L) baking dish.

Combine bread crumbs and Gruyère; sprinkle on top of zucchini. Dot with remaining 1 tbsp (15 mL) butter. Bake for 20 minutes or until bubbly and brown.

gratin dauphinois

This is just a fancy name for scalloped potatoes or potato gratin ("gratin" means with a cheese or bread crumb topping). This make-ahead family-style dish is the ideal winter meal after a cold day outdoors. SERVES 6

INGREDIENTS

1 clove garlic, unpeeled, halved
1/4 cup (50 mL) plus 1 tbsp (15 mL) butter
1 cup (250 mL) scalded milk
Bouquet garni (parsley stems, thyme, bay leaf) tied in cheesecloth
1/2 tsp (2 mL) freshly grated nutmeg or ground nutmeg
2 lb (1 kg) boiling potatoes *(red, white or small Yukon Golds)*
Salt and pepper
1 cup (250 mL) grated Gruyère cheese *(4 oz/125 g)*

If you love gratins, like this potato one, it's worth getting an inexpensive mandoline (plastic ones work fine) so the prep is quick. For a milder flavour, replace half the Gruyère with Emmental. To make it lighter, use chicken stock instead of milk (but you won't get the creamy flavour and consistency!). For a flavour varia-tion, add sage and cooked bacon.

METHOD

Set a rack in the upper third of the oven and preheat oven to 400°F (200°C). Rub a 10-inch (3 L) oval baking dish with garlic. Smear dish with 1 tbsp (15 mL) butter.

In a saucepan, steep milk with bouquet garni for 10 minutes. Season milk with nutmeg.

Peel potatoes and slice them 1/8 inch (3 mm) thick on a mandoline. Line casserole dish with one layer of potatoes. Season with salt, pepper, dollops of butter and a sprinkling of cheese. Continue layering. Top final layer with remaining cheese. Discard bouquet garni and pour milk over top of potatoes.

Bake for 30 to 40 minutes, until milk is absorbed, potatoes are tender, dish is bubbling around edges and top is crispy and brown. Let sit for 10 minutes before serving.

grilled leeks with dijon cream

I love this side dish with a simple grilled chicken. The inspiration for this recipe came from Alice Waters's *Chez Panisse Menu Cookbook*. Waters is the person who best expresses the importance of celebrating food straight from the earth. This dish yields lots of sauce, so it can double up as a sauce for the chicken. You can also sear chicken breasts, finish cooking them in this sauce and serve on angel hair pasta as a one-dish mid-week main. SERVES 8 TO 10

INGREDIENTS

10 leeks
2 tbsp (30 mL) vegetable oil
2 shallots, minced
4 cloves garlic, minced
1 cup (250 mL) white wine
1 cup (250 mL) 35% cream
3 tbsp (50 mL) Dijon mustard
2 tbsp (25 mL) chopped fresh tarragon
Salt and pepper, to taste
1/4 cup (50 mL) grated Parmesan cheese *(optional)*

METHOD

Trim off root ends of leeks and cut off dark green part of leaves, leaving white and some light green part. In a pot of boiling salted water, blanch leeks 2 minutes or until they just soften. Drain and refresh in ice water. Pat dry. Cut leeks in half lengthwise.

Heat a grill pan to high. Using a pastry brush, brush cut side of leeks with 1 tbsp (15 mL) of the oil. Place leeks cut side down in the pan and cook for 3 to 5 minutes without touching them. Turn leeks over and grill the other side for another 2 to 3 minutes. Transfer leeks to a serving platter.

In a skillet over medium-high heat, heat remaining 1 tbsp (15 mL) vegetable oil until hot. Sauté shallots until golden brown (about 5 minutes). Add garlic and cook for another 3 minutes. Stir in wine and cook until liquid is reduced by half. Add cream and continue to cook until cream has reduced by half and is thickened. Stir in Dijon and tarragon and season with salt and pepper. Pour sauce over leeks and top with Parmesan cheese. Serve immediately or keep warm for up to 30 minutes.

marinated grilled vegetables

When the weather warms up and barbecue season officially arrives, think of grilling spring vegetables such as asparagus and baby leeks. When fall comes, throw root vegetables such as beets and sweet potatoes on the grill. In winter, vegetables such as fennel, zucchini and eggplant are delicious grilled (or roasted, if it's too cold out to grill) with olive oil and topped with chèvre. SERVES 4 TO 6

You can use any variety of vegetables that you want. Hearty lettuces like radicchio and endive grill beautifully, and starches like sweet potatoes pick up the grill flavour well. Let the seasons guide what you choose.

Try grilling fruits too (like in our pork tenderloin recipe on page 140)—peaches and pineapples pair nicely with pork and duck. Grilled fruits are delicious brushed with a butter, brown sugar and curry mix.

INGREDIENTS

1 bunch basil, roughly chopped

2 tbsp (25 mL) sherry vinegar or white wine vinegar

1/2 cup (125 mL) very good quality extra-virgin olive oil, plus additional
    for brushing and serving

Salt and pepper, to taste

1 fennel bulb, cut lengthwise in medium-thick slices

1 bunch asparagus, tough stem ends trimmed

3 large beets, baked, peeled and sliced into rounds

METHOD

Preheat grill to high.

In a blender or food processor, combine basil and vinegar. Pulse until combined. Add 1/2 cup (125 mL) of the olive oil and pulse to just combined. Season with salt and pepper.

Brush vegetables all over with olive oil. Season generously with salt and pepper. Grill vegetables in batches on hot grill until they are tender and have nice grill marks. Transfer vegetables to a large platter and drizzle with basil vinaigrette. Season again. Let sit at room temperature until the rest of the meal is ready.

To serve, place some of the vegetables on each plate and drizzle with olive oil.

roasted balsamic asparagus

Simple, elegant and a perfect flavour pairing, this looks gorgeous on the plate as the vegetable anchor. SERVES 6

INGREDIENTS

2 bunches asparagus

2 tbsp (25 mL) extra-virgin olive oil

2 tbsp (25 mL) good-quality balsamic vinegar *(optional)*

Salt and pepper, to taste

1/4 cup (50 mL) grated Parmigiano-Reggiano cheese

Asparagus is also delicious grilled.

To simplify this dish even further, you can leave out the vinegar.

METHOD

Preheat oven to 450°F (220°C). Trim ends from asparagus and peel bottom third of stems. Place asparagus in a single layer on a baking sheet. Drizzle with olive oil and generously season with salt and pepper. Bake for 6 to 7 minutes or until almost tender.

Turn oven up to 500°F (260°C). Drizzle asparagus with balsamic vinegar and sprinkle with Parmesan cheese. Bake 2 more minutes, until cheese has melted.

beet hearts with chèvre

When we filmed *party dish*, our "romantic dinner for two" episode, starring my brother Robbie and his girlfriend (now wife!), had Robbie using a heart-shaped cookie cutter to cut the beets. You could drop the romance and corniness and just serve the food as it's meant to be!

SERVES 6

This is really about roasting your veg in their jackets instead of boiling and losing some of their colour and flavour.

This is one of my favourite salad combos and it's also great as a simple amuse-bouche to serve when guests are first seated, or as a casual antipasto.

Another roasted veg favourite is cauliflower—cut into large florets, season with salt and pepper, drizzle with good olive oil and roast on a baking sheet at 400°F (200°C) until tender and golden. A wonderful side as is or the start to our cauliflower soup (page 93).

INGREDIENTS
6 medium yellow and red beets
1/2 cup (125 mL) crumbled chèvre
3 tbsp (50 mL) chopped fresh chives
2 tbsp (25 mL) good-quality balsamic vinegar

METHOD
Preheat oven to 400°F (200°C). Wrap beets in foil, place on a baking sheet and roast for 1 hour or until soft in the centre. Peel skins off beets by rubbing with your fingers (wear rubber gloves) or with a paper towel. Slice beets into rounds about 1/4 inch (0.5 cm) thick. With a small heart-shaped cookie cutter, cut out heart shapes from beet slices, if desired. Arrange on plates and top with crumbled chèvre and chopped chives. Drizzle with balsamic vinegar.

slow-roasted tomatoes

These tomatoes are wonderful as a stand-alone side or in pastas, on pizzas or in a relish to accompany your favourite meat. Make a double batch and keep them in your fridge for several days, covered with a bit of olive oil.

INGREDIENTS

10 plum tomatoes, cut in half lengthwise
1/4 cup (50 mL) olive oil
Salt and freshly ground pepper, to taste

METHOD

Preheat oven to 300°F (150°C). Place tomatoes on a medium baking sheet. Drizzle with oil and season with salt and pepper. Toss until well coated. Arrange tomatoes cut side up in an even layer and bake for 2 to 3 hours, or until tomatoes are shrivelled but not too dry.

Don't scrimp on the salt in this recipe—salt helps to draw out the moisture. We like kosher or sea salt.

This recipe can also be made with grape or cherry tomatoes. Bake at 275°F (140°C) for 1 hour.

If you are in a hurry, crank up the oven to 450°F (230°C) and roast for 20 minutes.

sautéed winter greens

A quick and delicious way to get your dark greens, this side is a great accompaniment to your favourite meat dish. SERVES 12

To add a twist to this recipe, include slivered almonds and brown butter, sun-dried tomatoes and feta or a classic gremolata (minced lemon zest, garlic and parsley).

Chard, kale and rapini (otherwise known as broccoli rabe) are all excellent sources of vitamins A and C and iron. Chard is a member of the beet family, and kale and rapini the cabbage family, so all have deep earthy flavours that stand up perfectly with our steak au poivre (page 160) and beef tenderloin (page 158).

INGREDIENTS

3 tbsp (50 mL) olive oil

4 shallots, sliced

3 cloves garlic, minced

6 cups (1.5 L) your choice of baby spinach,
    Swiss chard, kale or rapini *(remove stems and centre
    rib from larger leaves and cut leaves in half if necessary)*

A few pinches dried chili flakes

Salt and pepper, to taste

1 1/2 tsp (7 mL) lemon juice

1 cup (250 mL) pine nuts, toasted

METHOD

In a large sauté pan or soup pot, heat oil over medium-high heat. Add shallots and garlic and sauté until soft. Add greens, chili flakes, salt and pepper and lemon juice. If using baby spinach, remove from heat and stir until just wilted. Sauté chard or kale until just wilted (about 2 minutes); sauté rapini a few minutes more. Transfer to serving platter and garnish with toasted pine nuts.

spicy broccolini

Broccolini is sometimes called baby broccoli. You could also use rapini.
These flavourful, somewhat bitter greens are hearty and very good for
you. A nice finish is toasted sesame seeds. Serve with your favourite fish
or grilled meat. SERVES 4

INGREDIENTS

2 or 3 bunches broccolini
3 tbsp (50 mL) olive oil
1 clove garlic, sliced
1/4 tsp (1 mL) chili flakes, or to taste
Kosher salt, to taste

METHOD

Remove and discard tough stems from broccolini. Cut broccolini into small florets
with some stem attached. Fill a large bowl with ice water and set aside. Bring a
large pot of salted water to a boil. Add broccolini; cook for 4 minutes after water
returns to a boil, or until almost tender and still green. Drain and place in ice water
to stop cooking. Drain again and set aside until ready to use.

In a medium sauté pan, heat oil over medium-high heat. Add garlic and heat
until fragrant but not browning. Add broccolini, chili flakes and salt. Sauté
until heated through.

twice-baked sweet potatoes with sage and pecans

One of our dish chefs, Kristin Donovan, served up this side in a class when the winter chilled us and we needed true comfort food! SERVES 8

The skins can be stuffed but not baked a few hours ahead of time and kept at room temp. Simply re-heat for 20 minutes before serving.

INGREDIENTS

8 medium sweet potatoes *(about 5 lb/2.5 kg)*
2 tbsp (25 mL) olive oil, plus more for roasting
Kosher salt and freshly ground pepper, to taste
1 head garlic
1/3 cup (75 mL) sour cream
3 tsp (15 mL) chopped fresh sage *(or your favourite fresh herb)*
1/4 cup (50 mL) chopped pecans

METHOD

Preheat oven to 450°F (230°C). Use a fork to prick holes in sweet potatoes; rub potatoes lightly with some olive oil and sprinkle with salt; place them on a baking sheet. Bake until fork tender (about 1 hour). Let cool slightly.

Halfway through baking potatoes, slice the top off the head of garlic, just enough to expose tops of cloves. Drizzle lightly with olive oil, wrap in foil and roast for 30 minutes in the oven along with the potatoes or until garlic is fragrant, browned and tender. Let cool slightly.

Reduce oven temperature to 375°F (190°C).

Slice sweet potatoes in half lengthwise. Remove and discard skin from 8 halves. Place potato flesh in a medium bowl. Use a spoon or melon baller to scoop out insides of the other 8 halves, leaving skins intact and enough of an edge to support the skins, and add flesh to bowl.

Squeeze 3 or 4 cloves roasted garlic *(save remaining garlic for another use)* into a small bowl and mash with a fork. Add sour cream, 2 tsp (10 mL) of the sage, salt and pepper; combine until smooth. Taste and adjust seasoning. Add mixture to sweet potato flesh, and mash with a potato masher or fork until well combined but still chunky.

Spoon mixture into skins; sprinkle with chopped pecans, remaining 1 tsp (5 mL) sage and a little hit of salt. Arrange on a baking sheet. Bake until potatoes are warmed and pecans are toasted (about 20 minutes). Serve immediately.

white vegetable purée

This is a dish cooking class favourite. Gillian Talacko, one of our chef-teachers, popularized this souped-up starch packed with flavour. It has evolved through the years. This will become a side mainstay in your house. SERVES 6

INGREDIENTS

3 sprigs fresh thyme

3 sprigs fresh parsley

1 bay leaf

2 large baking potatoes *(about 2 1/2 lb/1.25 kg)*, peeled and cubed

6 cloves garlic, peeled

2 lb (1 kg) celery root *(celeriac)*, peeled and cubed

3 medium turnips, peeled and cubed

3 leeks *(white part only)*, cut into 1-inch (2.5 cm) pieces

1/4 cup (50 mL) 35% cream

1 tbsp (15 mL) butter

1 tbsp (15 mL) grated fresh horseradish

2 tsp (10 mL) kosher salt

METHOD

Place thyme, parsley and bay leaf in a 5-inch (12 cm) square of cheesecloth. Tie corners of bouquet garni together with kitchen twine, leaving ends long enough to tie to pot handle.

Place potatoes and garlic in a large saucepan of cold well-salted water. Bring to a boil. Reduce heat to medium and cook, covered, until fork tender (about 25 minutes). Drain. Mash potatoes and garlic with ricer or masher. Transfer to a bowl.

Meanwhile, in a separate saucepan of boiling salted water, tie bouquet garni to handle of pot and immerse it in the water. Add celery root, turnips and leeks and cook, over medium-high heat, until tender (about 25 minutes). Drain (discarding bouquet garni) and transfer to a food processor. Pulse until smooth. Fold into potatoes with cream, butter, horseradish and salt. Serve immediately.

You say celeriac, I say celery root. It's ugly and knobby, varies in size and tastes like strong celery. Buy firm and refrigerate. If not using right away, peel and hold in water with lemon to prevent browning. Celeriac tastes great fresh, finely sliced in salads, cooked in soups or added to mashed potatoes for a delicious side dish.

Fresh horseradish is worth the hunt. You may need to hit a specialty produce store. It looks like a thick, woody stalk. Don't bother peeling it—simply use a Microplane grater, which will get you right down into the inside. After you use fresh horseradish, you'll never go back to the bottled stuff with your roast beef dinners.

desserts

Growing up we learned to expect dessert. My mom loves to bake and we were the lucky recipients of cakes and cookies at every meal. But in our time-pressed lives homebaked goodies seem to appear only on weekends, summer holidays or special occasions.

I could live on desserts. If I had my way, I would have chocolate and sweets morning, noon and night. I have so many favourite desserts, it was hard to pare them down, so these are truly my favourites. Some are very old—they tend to be the more casual and everyday (like the Spanish Cake and Stewie's Carrot Cake)—and some are newer, and typically more elegant (like the Lime Curd Tartlets). Many of the Special Occasion desserts lend themselves to fun presentation, like the Mini Cheesecakes. Restaurant favourites like Crème Brûlée are included to show you just how easy they are to do at home (and why we love them so much!).

There are so many different styles of baking and desserts, but good old-fashioned Canadian desserts are my favourite. I look to old Canadian cookbooks like our *Cottage Cookbook* for inspiration, but my grandmother's recipes (some of which, in turn, are her mother's) trump all—try the Buttermilk Chocolate Cake and the Chocolate Upside-down Cake, which are so straightforward, even my son, Findlay, helps bake them, and so popular they appear at every family birthday gathering.

EVERYDAY SIMPLE

cheater orange grapefruit sorbet

baked fruit with raspberry wine

mocha tortoni mousse

mocha brownies

butter tart squares

spanish cake with maple cream icing

chocolate upside-down cake

buttermilk chocolate cake

stewie's carrot cake

cheater orange grapefruit sorbet

Our talented pastry chef Charmaine Baan creates ice creams and desserts daily in the summer for our café and catering clients. There's always a fight between the kids and the staff for this refreshing sorbet. We call this a "cheater" sorbet because you don't need an ice-cream machine. MAKES ABOUT 4 CUPS (1 L)

This is my newest favourite (and that's coming from a chocoholic!). It's so refreshing and packed with the perfect flavour balance.

For a backyard fête, after processing, transfer sorbet into popsicle containers and serve homemade popsicles to guests!

This is the perfect base for any "ice" variation.

INGREDIENTS

2 large red grapefruits
3 oranges
1 lemon
1 cup (250 mL) sugar
1 cup (250 mL) water

METHOD

Zest enough of the grapefruit and oranges to get 1 tbsp (15 mL) zest from each. Set aside.

Juice grapefruits, oranges and lemon; strain juice through a fine-mesh sieve set over a large bowl. Set aside.

In a small saucepan over medium heat, stir together sugar, water and reserved zest. Bring to a boil, reduce heat and simmer for 3 minutes. Let cool. Strain syrup through fine-mesh sieve into strained juices. Stir to combine. Pour into a shallow metal pan, cover with foil and freeze for 3 or 4 hours, until almost firm.

Once firm, break up into chunks. Transfer to a food processor in 3 batches and purée until smooth and starting to foam. Transfer to an airtight container and freeze for 1 hour, until firm.

Before serving, let sorbet soften in refrigerator for 20 minutes.

baked fruit with raspberry wine

This is a classic French dessert. It may seem like a shame to cook beautiful fresh fruits when they are local and in season, but it is a gorgeous dish. If you can't bear to cook your fresh raspberries, make this dish in the off-season with less impressive berries and fruits. SERVES 6 TO 8

This dessert can turn quickly into a simple crumble. To make a ginger crumble, crush graham crumbs, add oats, butter, finely chopped crystallized ginger and brown sugar; crumble on top. Don't stir the fruit during baking.

Our liquor store shelves are stocked with gems for cooking. Framboise (raspberry wine) is one of them. Use on baked fruit or in a Canadian version of a kir royale—framboise and bubbly—my favourite signature welcome drink at a party.

INGREDIENTS

1 tbsp (15 mL) unsalted butter, for preparing baking dish
2 lb (1 kg) mixed fresh fruits *(figs, peaches, nectarines, apricots, plums)*
1 qt (1 L) blueberries
1 qt (1 L) raspberries
1 vanilla bean
1/2 cup (125 mL) raspberry dessert wine *(try Ontario's Southbrook Farms)*
2 tbsp (25 mL) lavender honey *(or honey of your choice)*, warmed
1/2 tsp (2 mL) cinnamon

METHOD

Preheat oven to 375°F (190°C). Generously butter a 10-inch (3 L) oval baking dish.
Quarter figs. Cut peaches, nectarines, apricots and plums into 1-inch (2.5 cm) wedges. Loosely arrange fruit, cut side up, in baking dish, slightly overlapping. Scatter mixed berries on top. Split vanilla bean lengthwise and scrape seeds onto fruits. Drizzle with raspberry dessert wine and honey; sprinkle with cinnamon.
Bake until fruits are plump and tender (about 20 minutes), carefully stirring once. Serve warm with ice cream.

mocha tortoni mousse

Quick, delicious and impressive and can be frozen for weeks!
Serve in a straight-sided glass bowl or trifle bowl or individual ramekins.
SERVES 8 TO 10

INGREDIENTS
2 large egg whites
2 tbsp (25 mL) instant coffee
Pinch salt
3/4 cup (175 mL) sugar
2 cups (500 mL) 35% cream
2 tsp (10 mL) vanilla
1/2 cup (125 mL) sugar
1/4 cup (50 mL) slivered almonds, toasted, plus extra for garnish
2 oz (50 g) bittersweet chocolate, grated

METHOD
In a very clean medium bowl, beat egg whites until foamy. Add instant coffee and
salt; beat until combined. Gradually add 1/4 cup (50 mL) sugar and beat until soft
peaks form.
In a separate bowl, whip cream until soft peaks form. Beat in vanilla and 1/2 cup
(125 mL) sugar. Fold cream into egg white mixture.
Fold in 1/4 cup (50 mL) slivered almonds and transfer to a large glass bowl or
individual glasses. Freeze at least 2 hours.
Garnish with remaining slivered almonds and grated chocolate. For an extra garnish,
add Chocolate Espresso Shards (page 232).

My dad was the lucky taster
when we were testing many of
the recipes for this book. He
voted to remove the nuts in this
mousse. If you prefer, use them
as a garnish only.

TOASTING NUTS
Whenever a recipe calls for nuts,
it is always best to dry toast them
to bring out flavour. Toast them in
a single layer on a baking sheet
in a 350°F (180°C) oven or in a dry
frying pan, stirring occasionally.
When the nuts become fragrant,
the natural oils are released. Allow
them to get light brown, then let
them cool. You can store toasted
nuts in an airtight container for a
few days.

mocha brownies

When we opened dish, we quickly became known for our fudgy brownies. Adell Shneer, a wonderful baker both at dish and with *party dish*, held the secret card to our favourite brownies. Then Charmaine Baan came along and developed a fantastic brownie that is now our café standard. This is the best combination of Adell's and Charmaine's secrets.

MAKES 12 LARGE OR 24 MINI BROWNIES

"Like water for chocolate"—ever wonder what that phrase meant (saw the movie and still didn't get it)? When chocolate is being melted, any amount of water in the chocolate will make it seize. (Don't ask. It's ugly and you'll have to start over.) Chocolate doesn't like moisture, so don't keep it in the fridge—best to keep in a cool, dark, dry place.

There are two camps when it comes to brownies—fudge brownies and cake brownies. If you fall into the fudge camp, you have found heaven with this recipe.

Once brownies have cooled, using a small round cookie cutter, cut into rounds and skewer onto popsicle sticks for brownie lollipops. Serve them with warm chocolate and dulce de leche dipping sauces, if you like.

INGREDIENTS

1 cup (250 mL) all-purpose flour
1 tbsp (15 mL) instant espresso powder
1/4 tsp (1 mL) salt
6 oz (175 g) bittersweet chocolate, chopped
2 oz (60 g) unsweetened chocolate, chopped
3/4 cup (175 mL) unsalted butter, cubed
1 1/2 cups (375 mL) sugar
2 1/2 tsp (12 mL) vanilla
4 large eggs
3/4 cup (175 mL) semi-sweet chocolate chips

METHOD

Preheat oven to 350°F (180°C). Butter a 13- x 9-inch (3 L) baking pan and line with parchment paper (or grease pan and dust with flour).

In a small bowl, combine flour, espresso powder and salt. Set aside.

In a medium heatproof bowl over a pot of barely simmering water, melt bittersweet chocolate, unsweetened chocolate and butter together, stirring occasionally. (Make sure no water touches the chocolate.) Remove from heat and add sugar and vanilla; stir with a wooden spoon or spatula until smooth. Stir in eggs, one at a time, until incorporated. Fold in flour mixture. Stir in chocolate chips.

Spread in prepared pan and bake for 25 to 30 minutes, or until set but a few crumbs stick to tester when inserted. Let cool on a rack.

butter tart squares

This non-pastry butter tart square is about the yummiest I have come across! My family voted for the gooier, no-nuts version (you can add more raisins). When Michelle makes these in the café, they never last long.

MAKES 20 TO 24 SQUARES

This recipe doubles very well—double all ingredients and cook in an 18- x 12-inch (46 x 30 cm) rimmed baking sheet.

INGREDIENTS

Base

2 cups (500 mL) all-purpose flour
1/2 cup (125 mL) granulated sugar
1 cup (250 mL) cold unsalted butter, cut into cubes

Topping

1/4 cup (50 mL) unsalted butter, melted and cooled
4 large eggs, lightly beaten
2 cups (500 mL) packed brown sugar
1/4 cup (50 mL) all-purpose flour
1/4 cup (50 mL) corn syrup
1 tsp (5 mL) baking powder
1 tsp (5 mL) vanilla
1/4 tsp (1 mL) salt
2 cups (500 mL) golden raisins
1 cup (250 mL) pecans, coarsely chopped (optional)

METHOD

Preheat oven to 350°F (180°C). Line an 8-inch (2 L) square pan with parchment paper and grease the paper.

To make the base, in a large bowl, combine flour and sugar. Using two knives or a pastry blender, cut in butter until mixture is the texture of coarse meal. Press firmly into the baking pan, going slightly up the sides of the pan. Bake for 15 to 20 minutes, until just slightly golden.

To make the topping, in a large bowl, stir together butter and eggs. Add sugar, flour, corn syrup, baking powder, vanilla and salt; stir until combined. Fold in raisins and pecans. Pour over base and bake for an additional 20 to 25 minutes or until top springs back when touched.

Let cool on a rack. When cool, cover and refrigerate overnight before cutting into squares.

spanish cake with maple cream icing

When I was a private chef for Martin Short's family one summer in Muskoka, they were hosting the Hankses and the Spielbergs. It was Tom Hanks's birthday and he had only two requests—a Canadian celebration and this Spanish cake! SERVES 6

If this is a casual family gathering, ice the cake in the pan. If you're entertaining, line the pan with parchment paper and, when cool, turn the cake out onto a platter and ice top and sides.

It's a toss-up in our family which is the most coveted cake—this or the upside-down cake on page 207. It's really all about the icing. This cake comes from my mom and grand-mother's hometown of Winnipeg. I am still waiting to hear why it's called Spanish cake!

INGREDIENTS

1 cup (250 mL) all-purpose flour
1 tsp (5 mL) baking powder
1 tsp (5 mL) cinnamon
1/2 cup (125 mL) butter, at room temperature
1 cup (250 mL) sugar
2 large eggs, separated
1/2 cup (125 mL) milk

Icing

1/4 cup (50 mL) butter, melted
1/2 cup (125 mL) brown sugar
2 tbsp (25 mL) milk
1 cup (250 mL) icing sugar

METHOD

Preheat oven to 350°F (180°C). Butter an 8-inch (2 L) square cake pan.

Sift together flour, baking powder and cinnamon. Set aside.

In a large bowl, beat butter with sugar until fluffy. In a separate bowl, lightly beat egg yolks. Beat yolks into butter mixture.

Add flour mixture to butter mixture alternately with milk in 3 to 5 parts, ending with flour mixture.

In a separate, very clean bowl, beat egg whites until soft peaks form. Gently fold egg whites into batter.

Spoon batter into pan and bake for 25 to 30 minutes or until cake springs back when touched, top is light golden and cake starts to pull away from edges of pan. Cool completely on a rack before icing.

To make icing, in a medium saucepan, melt butter. Add brown sugar; simmer, stirring, for 2 minutes. Stir in milk. Bring to a boil, stirring. Let cool. Stir in icing sugar.

chocolate upside-down cake

This is the most famous dessert among the young visitors to my mother's table. Friends call my mom ahead with a special request for it. My three brothers and I would always battle over seconds of this cake. To save the fight, this recipe makes two cakes! SERVES 10

INGREDIENTS

2 cups (500 mL) all-purpose flour

1 1/2 cups (375 mL) sugar

3 tbsp (50 mL) cocoa powder

1 tbsp (15 mL) baking powder

1 tsp (5 mL) salt

1 cup (250 mL) milk

1/4 cup (50 mL) butter, melted

2 tsp (10 mL) vanilla

Sauce

1 cup (250 mL) brown sugar

1 cup (250 mL) granulated sugar

1/4 cup (50 mL) cocoa powder

2 cups (500 mL) hot water

This cake is called "upside-down" because the hot sauce is poured over the top and after baking ends up on the bottom. This is a messy and tricky cake to turn out, so just cut pieces and flip over onto plates so the sauce is back on top.

This is a pantry essentials cake that requires no fancy ingredients, just the baking basics.

You can easily halve the recipe and cook in one 8-inch (2 L) square pan. Serves 4 to 6.

METHOD

Preheat oven to 350°F (180°C). Grease two 8-inch (2 L) square cake pans.

Into a large bowl, sift together flour, sugar, cocoa powder, baking powder and salt. Stir in milk, butter and vanilla until well blended. Divide batter between pans and set aside while you make the sauce.

In a heavy saucepan over medium-high heat, bring sauce ingredients to a boil, stirring. Boil sauce for 5 minutes, stirring, making a thin syrup. Pour sauce over batter.

Bake for 40 minutes or until top of cake springs back when touched and sides pull away from the pan. Serve warm with a dollop of whipped cream or vanilla ice cream.

buttermilk chocolate cake

This old-fashioned one-bowl chocolate cake is four generations old and a staple in our household for most celebrations. It's the fastest, easiest surefire cake for a last-minute dessert. Freda Woods is a friend of my grandmother, and when my brother met Freda he said, "*You* are Freda Woods? You're famous!" Both Findlay and Olivia enjoyed chocolate for the first time with this as their first birthday cake (mini cupcakes!).

SERVES 8 TO 10

Buttermilk is one of those ingredients you buy for one recipe and then cannot figure out what to do with the rest. Use it up in pancakes or in a batter for fried chicken or in our Cool Roasted Red Pepper and Buttermilk Soup (page 85).

If you are serving this icing to kids, you can replace the coffee with buttermilk.

You can make half this recipe in one pan for a single-layer cake.

Spread leftover icing on graham wafers.

INGREDIENTS

2 large eggs
2 cups (500 mL) buttermilk *(approx.)*
2 cups (500 mL) all-purpose flour
2 cups (500 mL) sugar
1/2 cup (125 mL) cocoa powder
2 tsp (10 mL) baking soda
1 tsp (5 mL) baking powder
1/2 tsp (2 mL) salt
1 cup (250 mL) vegetable oil
2 tsp (10 mL) vanilla

METHOD

Preheat oven to 350°F (180°C). Generously grease (or grease and line with parchment paper) two 8-inch (1.2 L) or 9-inch (1.5 L) round cake pans.

In a 2-cup (500 mL) measuring cup, lightly beat eggs. Add enough buttermilk to measure 2 cups (500 mL).

With an electric mixer on low speed, stir together flour, sugar, cocoa powder, baking soda, baking powder and salt. Slowly add oil, egg-and-buttermilk mixture and vanilla. Increase speed to medium-high and beat for 2 minutes, until well combined.

Divide batter between cake pans and bake for 30 to 40 minutes or until tops are firm and tester comes out clean. Transfer to a rack and cool completely. When cool, slide a thin knife around outside of pans and turn cakes out onto rack.

Place 1 cake layer on a cake plate. Using an offset spatula, ice top of cake. Carefully place the second cake layer on top. Ice top and sides completely.

icing

INGREDIENTS

1/2 cup (125 mL) butter, melted
1/2 cup (125 mL) cocoa powder
4 cups (1 L) icing sugar
1/4 cup (50 mL) strong brewed coffee *(or to desired consistency)*

METHOD

Beat all ingredients in bowl of an electric mixer for a minute until creamy. Adjust the amount of any ingredient to your own desired consistency.
This yields a lot of icing. I like to err on the side of caution (and sampling).

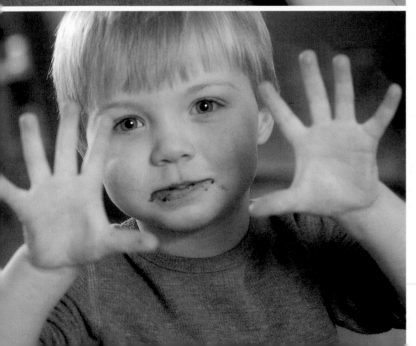

icing

INGREDIENTS

4 oz (125 g) cream cheese, softened *(you can use light)*

1/4 cup (50 mL) unsalted butter, softened

2 cups (500 mL) icing sugar

1 tbsp (15 mL) reserved pineapple juice *(approx.)*

METHOD

In a large bowl, beat cream cheese until soft. Add butter and continue beating until well blended. Beat in icing sugar, 1 cup (250 mL) at a time, until icing is smooth, scraping sides of bowl as necessary. Add up to 1 tbsp (15 mL) pineapple juice to thin icing slightly.

This cake is best on day 2 or 3!

This cake recipe can be doubled. The icing recipe can be doubled (or tripled or quadrupled!) and stored in the fridge. Since this is a casual cake that yields a large amount and usually lasts a few days, I leave the cake in the pan and serve pieces as need be.

---

stewie's carrot cake

Stewie, my mom's great friend and one of my key recipe testers, provided this recipe as well as inspiration for many others. Her original recipe doesn't have raisins—a perfect example of how recipes get adapted and changed from person to person. Stewie's famous carrot cake became our dish café signature cake, and we kept the recipe top secret. Well, here it is—revealed! SERVES 12

INGREDIENTS

2 cups (500 mL) sugar

1 1/2 cups (375 mL) vegetable oil

3 large eggs

1 tsp (5 mL) vanilla

2 1/2 cups (625 mL) all-purpose flour

1 tsp (5 mL) baking soda

1 tsp (5 mL) cinnamon

1/2 tsp (2 mL) kosher salt

2 cups (500 mL) grated carrots *(approx. 4 large)*

1 cup (250 mL) golden raisins

1 cup (250 mL) drained crushed pineapple *(save the juice)*

METHOD

Preheat oven to 350°F (180°C). Line a 13- x 9-inch (3 L) cake pan with parchment paper.

In a medium bowl, beat together sugar and vegetable oil. Add eggs, one at a time, beating well after each addition, and beat until light and fluffy. Beat in vanilla.

In a separate bowl, stir together flour, baking soda, cinnamon and salt.

Put grated carrots, raisins and drained pineapple in a large bowl. Fold in egg mixture until well blended. Fold in flour mixture until well blended.

Pour batter into cake pan and bake for 50 to 60 minutes or until a tester comes out clean. Let cake cool in pan.

SPECIAL OCCASIONS

caramelized pears with mascarpone cream

mini meringue cups with rhubarb compote

mini white chocolate and raspberry cheesecakes

molten chocolate lava cakes with caramel sauce

frozen lemon soufflé

chocolate pots

crème brûlée

sticky toffee puddings

lime curd tartlets

espresso granita

chocolate espresso shards

fresh raspberry coulis

caramelized pears with mascarpone cream

Martha Mansfield, one of my dedicated recipe testers and an avid cook, fell in love with this recipe. It quickly became her family's Sunday night dessert favourite. Poached pears are elegant, and when paired with mascarpone, they create a dessert that is lovely and sophisticated. Whether you poach a whole pear or pear halves, the caramelized sweetness and beauty on the plate is a force to be reckoned with. You can leave the skins on or remove them. SERVES 4

The mascarpone cream can be made a few days ahead. Keep covered and refrigerated.

You can make this with larger pears, such as Bartlett, Bosc or Anjou. Use a large sauté pan. You might have to finish cooking them on a parchment-lined baking sheet in a 375°F (190°C) oven for 5 to 20 minutes after removing from the sauté pan.

INGREDIENTS

1/2 cup (125 mL) 35% cream
1/2 cup (125 mL) mascarpone cheese
2 tbsp (25 mL) granulated sugar
4 mini pears, such as Forelle
2 tbsp (25 mL) unsalted butter
2 tbsp (25 mL) honey
1/2 vanilla bean, split in half lengthwise

2 pieces star anise
2 cardamom pods
1/2 cinnamon stick
1/4 tsp (1 mL) freshly grated nutmeg
2 tbsp (25 mL) brown sugar
4 tsp (20 mL) fresh lemon juice

METHOD

In a bowl, beat together cream, mascarpone and granulated sugar until soft peaks form. Refrigerate until ready to use.

Peel pears if desired, leaving stem attached, and cut in half lengthwise. Remove cores with a melon baller. Set aside.

In a small sauté pan over medium heat, melt butter with honey. Add vanilla bean, star anise, cardamom, cinnamon and nutmeg. Heat until mixture is foamy, about 1 minute. Add pears, cut side down, and reduce heat to medium-low. Cook pears until golden brown and tender (test with a sharp knife), 10 to 12 minutes. Stir in brown sugar and lemon juice and cook until mixture is syrupy, 1 to 2 minutes. Transfer pears to plates. Remove spices from syrup. Serve pears warm with a dollop of mascarpone cream and a drizzle of syrup.

mini meringue cups with rhubarb compote

My grandmother (*grandmère* of baking) claims that meringues must be made on a dry day. If it's raining—postpone. She knows! Fill with our Lime Curd (page 230) or this flavourful Rhubarb Compote.
MAKES 36 MINI CUPS

These mini meringue cups can also be made as little kisses. Using a piping bag fitted with a small or medium ribbed tip, twist a little kiss onto parchment paper. Alternatively, make traditional pavlova. No piping bag required! Spoon 1/4 cup (50 mL) of meringue mixture onto parchment and carefully swirl and flatten into a nest. Once cooked and cooled, serve with fresh whipped cream and seasonal berries.

INGREDIENTS
4 large egg whites
1/4 tsp (1 mL) salt
1/4 tsp (1 mL) cream of tartar
1 cup (250 mL) sugar

METHOD
Preheat oven to 250°F (120°C). Line 2 baking sheets with parchment paper.

In bowl of an electric mixer, beat egg whites until foamy. Add salt and cream of tartar; whip until soft peaks form. Gradually add sugar, beating at high speed until whites hold stiff, glossy peaks.

Spoon meringue into a pastry bag fitted with a medium plain tip; pipe cups, starting with a 2-inch (5 cm) wide base and coiling a rope around the edge of the base twice to make sides.

Bake meringues for 1 1/2 hours, turning heat down to 225°F (110°C) if they begin to brown. Allow meringues to cool in oven with heat off and door slightly ajar. Store cooled meringues in an airtight tin.

rhubarb compote

This compote is a spring dessert staple.
It is a wonderful way to dress up vanilla
ice cream. MAKES 2 CUPS (500 ML)

INGREDIENTS

8 stalks rhubarb, cut into 1/4-inch (0.5 cm) pieces
   (or 4 cups/1 L frozen)
3/4 cup (175 mL) sugar
1/4 cup (50 mL) white wine
1/4 cup (50 mL) port
1/4 cup (50 mL) orange juice
1 cinnamon stick
1 vanilla bean, split in half lengthwise
3 cardamom pods
3 pieces lemon peel
Fresh mint, for garnish

METHOD

In a medium saucepan, combine rhubarb, sugar,
   wine, port, orange juice, cinnamon stick, vanilla
   bean, cardamom pods and lemon peel. Bring
   to a boil over medium-high heat, stirring occasionally. Reduce heat to medium-low, cover and
   simmer for 10 to 12 minutes or until mixture
   thickens slightly. Transfer to a bowl and cool.
Fill meringue cups with Rhubarb Compote and top
   with fresh mint.

mini white chocolate and raspberry cheesecakes

My *party dish* wing-women Andrea Paric and Adell Shneer concocted these adorable and delicious creations for a specialty coffee and dessert party. They remind me of my Queen's University days when my roommates Kristi and Lynn and I managed to wrangle the secrets to the perfect cheesecake from the (now-defunct) Chinese Laundry Café.

MAKES 24 MINI CHEESECAKES

For presentation in entertaining, when it comes to desserts, I love everything mini. Little morsels allow for more variety and let you eat more, without eating more!

For this photo, we topped each mini cheesecake with a spoonful of dulce de leche and then added a raspberry.

INGREDIENTS

Crust

5 oz (150 g) butter cookies or shortbread (*about 40 cookies*)
1/4 cup (50 mL) unsalted butter, melted

Filling

1 1/2 pkg (375 g) cream cheese, softened
1/3 cup (75 mL) sugar
2 large eggs
1 tsp (5 mL) vanilla
2 oz (60 g) good-quality white chocolate, chopped
1/2 pint (250 mL) blackberries or raspberries

METHOD

Preheat oven to 375°F (190°C). Place 2 silicone mini muffin trays (each with 12 mini muffin cups) or a well-greased muffin tray on a baking sheet.

In a food processor, pulse cookies into fine crumbs. Add melted butter and pulse to combine. Place 1/2 tbsp (7 mL) cookie crumbs in each muffin cup and tap down with a small spoon. Refrigerate while making filling.

In bowl of an electric mixer fitted with the paddle attachment, beat cream cheese until smooth; gradually beat in sugar until smooth. Add eggs, one at a time, beating well after each addition. Blend in vanilla.

In a heatproof bowl set over a pot of barely simmering water, melt chocolate. Slowly stir into cream cheese mixture.

Spoon about 1 tbsp (15 mL) cream cheese mixture into each muffin cup. Place a berry in the centre of each cup. Top with remaining mixture, filling cups to the top.

Bake for 15 to 18 minutes or until puffed and set. Let cool on a rack for 20 minutes. Remove from muffin cups by carefully pushing cakes from the bottom until they pop out. Let cool completely on a tray. (Centres will cave in slightly.) Refrigerate for at least an hour before serving. Garnish with fresh berries.

molten chocolate lava cakes with caramel sauce

This is my version of the popular restaurant favourite flourless chocolate cake . . . with a tiny bit of flour! SERVES 6

When you are making a dessert that's all about the chocolate, get the good stuff. As with coffee and wine, the producer is key. My favourites are Valrhona, Callebaut, Scharffen Berger and Lindt. Unadulterated chocolate is unsweetened (50 to 58% cocoa butter). Added sugar gives us bittersweet (35% chocolate liquor) and semi-sweet or sweet (15 to 35%). Milk chocolate, to which dry milk has been added, must have 10% chocolate liquor. The higher the cocoa count (as in unsweetened and bittersweet), the more intense the flavour. If you are a serious chocolate baker, replace that semi-sweet with bittersweet. (White chocolate is not true chocolate because it contains no chocolate liquor.)

INGREDIENTS

Lava Cakes

1/2 cup (125 mL) unsalted butter
6 oz (175 g) bittersweet chocolate, chopped
2 large eggs
2 large egg yolks
1/4 cup (50 mL) sugar
Pinch salt
2 tbsp (25 mL) all-purpose flour
Whipped cream, for serving

Caramel Sauce

1/2 cup (125 mL) sugar
1/2 cup (125 mL) 35% cream
2 tbsp (25 mL) brandy

METHOD

To make the Caramel Sauce, in a small, heavy saucepan, heat sugar over medium-high heat, without stirring or swirling, until it begins to turn an amber colour around the edges (about 7 minutes). Immediately remove pan from heat and carefully add cream and brandy (mixture will sputter). Return to heat and cook, stirring frequently until caramel melts. Set aside until serving. Mixture will thicken as it cools.

Preheat oven to 450°F (230°C). Butter and lightly flour 6 (1/2-cup/125 mL) ramekins. Tap out excess flour. Set ramekins on a baking sheet.

In a bowl set over a pot of barely simmering water, melt butter and chocolate. Whisk until smooth.

In bowl of an electric mixer fitted with the whisk attachment, beat eggs, egg yolks, sugar and salt until pale yellow and light. Quickly fold chocolate mixture into eggs. Fold in flour.

Spoon about 1/3 cup (75 mL) batter into each ramekin. Bake for 10 to 12 minutes or until the sides of the cakes are set and the centres are still soft. Let cakes cool in ramekins for 1 minute and then invert them onto dessert plates. Let ramekins stand for 10 seconds before lifting them off the cakes. Serve immediately with the caramel sauce and whipped cream.

frozen lemon soufflé

I collected some wonderful recipes from supportive catering clients in my early catering years. One client and wonderful cook asked me to prepare this recipe for her fundraiser. It quickly became one of my go-to warm weather favourites (thank you, Janet!). Originally jotted on scrap paper, this recipe has seen few revisions over the years. SERVES 12

This dessert can also be made into 12 individual soufflés and can be frozen for up to 2 weeks.

To speed up whipping cream, place beaters in freezer and cream in bowl in fridge.

INGREDIENTS

1 box (250 g) vanilla wafers
1/4 cup (50 mL) butter, melted
4 large eggs, separated
1/2 cup (125 mL) fresh lemon juice *(from 2 large lemons)*
1 1/2 tbsp (20 mL) lemon zest
3/4 cup (175 mL) plus 1/4 cup (50 mL) sugar
1/8 tsp (0.5 mL) cream of tartar
1/8 tsp (0.5 mL) salt
1 1/2 cups (375 mL) 35% cream
Lemon zest or candied lilacs, for garnish

METHOD

Crush wafers in a food processor. Drizzle in melted butter and process briefly to combine. Press firmly into bottom of a 9-inch (2.5 L) or 10-inch (3 L) springform pan.

In a large bowl, lightly beat egg yolks. Add lemon juice, lemon zest and 1/4 cup (50 mL) sugar; blend well.

In a separate, very clean bowl, beat egg whites until foamy. Beat in cream of tartar and salt. Continue beating until soft peaks form. Gradually add remaining 3/4 cup (175 mL) sugar and beat until stiff peaks form.

In a separate bowl, whip cream.

Fold egg whites and whipped cream into yolk mixture. Spoon into springform pan. Cover with foil. Freeze at least 8 hours.

Let soften in fridge for 30 minutes before serving. Remove sides from pan and decorate soufflé with lemon zest or candied violets.

crème brûlée

This is the classic restaurant favourite. When you recreate this dessert at home you will realize how straightforward it is. All it takes is the tempering skill, the cute little ramekins (used for so many elegant desserts) and a small blowtorch, which, if you have a responsible crowd, can add a fun interactive component to the party (in the kitchen, supervised, please!). Make this up to a day ahead and simply torch at the last minute. SERVES 8

Lavender (2 tbsp/25 mL of fresh or dried), hazelnut (1/4 cup/50 mL paste or 1/2 cup/125 mL ground) or lemongrass (2 fresh stems, chopped) are great additions to the custard in this classic dessert.

If you don't have a kitchen blowtorch, use the broiler. Place oven rack on top level. Leaving oven door slightly ajar, broil custards on a cookie sheet a few minutes or until sugar melts and just starts to blacken.

INGREDIENTS
4 cups (1 L) 35% cream
1 tbsp (15 mL) vanilla
9 large egg yolks
1 cup (250 mL) plus 1/4 cup (50 mL) sugar

METHOD
Preheat oven to 325°F (160°C). In a medium saucepan over medium-high heat, heat cream and vanilla just until bubbles begin to form around edge of saucepan. Remove from heat.

In a heatproof bowl, whisk egg yolks with 1 cup (250 mL) sugar until very pale. Whisking constantly, slowly pour hot cream into egg mixture, whisking gently until blended. Strain custard through a fine-mesh sieve into a bowl and divide among 8 (1/2-cup/125 mL) ramekins.

Place ramekins in a roasting pan. Carefully pour enough boiling water into pan to come halfway up the sides of the ramekins. Bake for 40 minutes or until just set around edges and centre jiggles. If custards are beginning to brown on top, cover loosely with foil.

Remove from water bath, let cool and refrigerate for at least 2 hours before serving.

Sprinkle each custard with about 1 tsp (5 mL) sugar, shaking gently to evenly spread sugar. Using kitchen blowtorch, caramelize tops until sugar bubbles and is amber in colour. Cool and serve.

sticky toffee puddings

The discovery of a sticky toffee pudding at my local Irish pub sent me on a quest for a recipe I could recreate. This one is adapted from *The Best of Bridge*, a classic oldie but goldie cookbook. SERVES 8

Dates are a great alternative to the dried cranberries.

INGREDIENTS

Pudding

1 1/4 cups (300 mL) water
1/2 tsp (2 mL) vanilla
1/2 tsp (2 mL) baking soda
1 cup (250 mL) dried cranberries
3/4 cup (175 mL) butter
2/3 cup (150 mL) granulated sugar
2 large eggs, lightly beaten
1 cup (250 mL) all-purpose flour
1/4 tsp (1 mL) baking powder

Toffee Sauce

1 cup (250 mL) brown sugar
1/2 cup (125 mL) butter
1/2 cup (125 mL) 35% cream

METHOD

Bring water to a boil. Add vanilla, baking soda and cranberries. Let cool.
Preheat oven to 350°F (180°C). Butter 8 (1/2-cup/125 mL) ramekins.
To make the puddings, with an electric mixer, cream butter and sugar until fluffy. Add eggs. Beat until combined.
Sift flour and baking powder together; fold into batter. Fold in wet cranberry mixture. Divide mixture evenly among ramekins. Bake for 25 minutes or until a toothpick comes out clean.
Meanwhile, make the Toffee Sauce. Combine sauce ingredients in a saucepan and stir over low heat until sugar is dissolved and sauce thickens.
Run a knife around edge of ramekins and invert puddings onto plates. Serve drizzled with toffee sauce.

lime curd tartlets

My sister-in-law Amanda has quickly become a keen cook and a fearless recipe tester. She decided to test this for our whole family at our remote family cottage. A power outage didn't stop her—she tried to cook the curd on top of the wood stove, and when that took too long, she moved to our makeshift charcoal barbecue. Not intended to be a campfire dish, this recipe can officially be cooked anywhere!

MAKES 16 MINI TARTLETS

Tart shells can be made 1 or 2 days ahead and stored in an air-tight container.

You can replace lime juice and zest with equal amounts of lemon or grapefruit.

Instead of phyllo, use 16 wonton wrappers.

INGREDIENTS

Lime Curd

3/4 cup (175 mL) sugar
1/4 cup (50 mL) unsalted butter
1/2 cup (125 mL) fresh lime juice
1 tbsp (15 mL) lime zest
1 1/2 tsp (7 mL) lemon zest
3 large eggs

Tartlets

3 sheets phyllo pastry
3 tbsp (50 mL) butter, melted
Icing sugar, for dusting
Berries and tiny mint sprigs, for garnish

METHOD

To make the Lime Curd, in a medium saucepan, combine sugar, butter, lime juice and zests. Cook over medium-high heat, stirring constantly, until butter is melted and sugar is dissolved (about 4 minutes).

In a heatproof bowl, whisk eggs. Continue whisking while slowly pouring in hot citrus liquid. Return egg mixture to saucepan and cook over medium-low heat, stirring constantly, until mixture thickens and coats the back of a spoon (about 5 minutes). Transfer to a bowl, cover surface directly with plastic wrap and cool in fridge until ready to serve.

To make the tart shells, preheat oven to 350°F (180°C). Lay 1 sheet of phyllo on a cutting board and brush liberally with melted butter. Lay a second sheet of phyllo over buttered sheet and brush with butter. Repeat with remaining phyllo sheet. Using a knife or cookie cutter, cut into sixteen 3-inch (8 cm) rounds or squares. Press phyllo into mini muffin tins. Bake 10 to 15 minutes, until golden. Let cool completely.

Spoon a dollop of curd into each tart shell. Top with fresh berries and tiny mint sprigs.

espresso granita

A nice refreshing "ice" on its own or accompanied by flavoured whipped cream (it will resemble a faux cappuccino!). SERVES 4

INGREDIENTS
4 cups (1 L) strong brewed coffee
1/2 cup (125 mL) sugar
Pinch of salt

Topping
1/2 cup (125 mL) chilled 35% cream
1 tsp (5 mL) vanilla
Cocoa and cinnamon, for dusting

METHOD
Bring coffee, sugar and salt to a boil over high heat. Boil 1 minute, until sugar dissolves. Let cool.

When coffee mixture is cool, add more sugar to taste, if desired. Pour mixture into a baking pan or casserole dish and freeze for 2 hours.

Using a fork, scrape ice into large chunks. Put into a food processor and pulse a few seconds until granita comes together and foams. Return to baking pan for at least 30 minutes and keep frozen until ready to serve.

Whip cream to soft peaks. Whip in vanilla. (This can be done a few hours ahead of time. Chill cream until needed.)

Spoon frozen granita into espresso cups (or sherry glasses). Top with a dollop of whipped cream. Dust top with cocoa and cinnamon.

dish dessert essentials

Here are a couple of recipes we can't live without. They dress up the simplest desserts and turn them into something truly special.

chocolate espresso shards

INGREDIENTS
6 oz (175 g) bittersweet chocolate
1/3 cup (75 mL) espresso beans

METHOD
Chop chocolate. Place chocolate in a heatproof bowl over a pot of barely simmering water. Make sure the water does not touch the bottom of the bowl. Stir until melted and smooth.

Use a coffee mill to coarsely grind espresso beans (or put them in a resealable plastic bag and pound them with the bottom of a small pan). Fold coffee into melted chocolate.

Pour chocolate mixture onto a parchment-lined baking sheet and use a metal spatula to spread to an even thickness. Chill until set. Break chocolate into shards.

Shards can be stored in the fridge, in an airtight container. Use to garnish any chocolate dessert for a little extra touch. Feel free to finely chop coffee beans if you prefer a more refined consistency.

fresh raspberry coulis
MAKES 2 CUPS (500 ML)

INGREDIENTS
2 pints (1 L) fresh raspberries
1/2 cup (125 mL) sugar *(or to taste depending on sweetness of fruit)*
2 tsp (10 mL) finely grated lemon zest
2 tbsp (25 mL) fresh lemon juice

METHOD
In a food processor, purée raspberries and sugar. Stir in lemon zest. Taste and add enough lemon juice to brighten the flavour without adding a strong lemon taste. Add more sugar if necessary.

Pour berry mixture through a fine-mesh strainer set over a bowl, pressing down with a spoon to force the fruit and juices through. Transfer to a nonaluminum container and refrigerate, covered, until ready to serve. The coulis will keep well for several days.

When raspberries aren't in season, use about 3 cups (750 mL) frozen berries.

INDEX

Note: "Variation" following an index entry refers to a variation of the recipe that can be found in its sidebar. Cheeses are listed by type (e.g., "feta cheese").

O

P